Poetry Explorers

Kent

Edited by Vivien Linton

First published in Great Britain in 2009 by

Remus House
Coltsfoot Drive
Peterborough
PE2 9JX
Telephone: 01733 890066
Website: www.youngwriters.co.uk

All Rights Reserved
Book Design by Spencer Hart
Illustrations by Ali Smith
© Copyright Contributors 2009
SB ISBN 978-1-84924-250-9

Foreword

At Young Writers our defining aim is to promote an enjoyment of reading and writing amongst children and young adults. By giving aspiring poets the opportunity to see their work in print, their love of the written word as well as confidence in their own abilities has the chance to blossom.

Our latest competition Poetry Explorers was designed to introduce primary school children to the wonders of creative expression. They were given free reign to write on any theme and in any style, thus encouraging them to use and explore a variety of different poetic forms.

We are proud to present the resulting collection of regional anthologies which are an excellent showcase of young writing talent. With such a diverse range of entries received, the selection process was difficult yet very rewarding. From comical rhymes to poignant verses, there is plenty to entertain and inspire within these pages. We hope you agree that this collection bursting with imagination is one to treasure.

Contents

Chiddingstone Primary School, Edenbridge

Molly Bradley (10) 1
Louise Roche (11) 2
Ellalute Shamwana (10) 3
Sophie Tyrrell (11) 4
Tom Wiles (10) 5
Jack Price (10) 6
Melissa Harper (10) 6
Charlotte Crofts-Bolster (10) 7

Eastry CE Primary School, Eastry

Anna Pullen (8) 7
Amy Sampson (9) 8
Lucy Rafferty (8) 8
Ellie Coupland (8) 9
Henry Armstrong (8) 9
Sam Cott (8) 10
Becky Baker (9) 10
Alicia Prestleton (9) 11
James Ball (8) 11
Emily Burton (9) 12

Grove Park Community School, Sittingbourne

Will Tumber (7) 12
Mai Tumber (9) 13
Emily Davis (9) 13
Olivia Holyoake (9) 14
Charlotte Quinn (8) 14
Eloisa Walsom (9) 15
Joe Matten (8) 15
Tara Winterbourn (9) 16
Cerys Demomme (9) 16
Renee Quartey-Peluola (8) 16

Long Mead CP School, Tonbridge

Jade Warner (11)
& Hannah Batchelor (10) 17

Luddenham School, Faversham

Ellie Turner (10) 18
Frank Radcliffe-Adams (10) 19
Hazel-Anne Frost (10) 20
Angus Clarke (10) 21
Christina Kenton (10) 22
Robyn Hilliard (10) 23
Daniel Klein (10) 24
Grace McGrath (10) 25
Harry Elliott Taylor (10) 26
Paige Sheaff (10) 27
Lilly-May Pilcher (11) 28
Jessica Childs (11) 29
Poppy Johnson (10) 30
Abbie Ramsden (10) 31
Emily Carter (10) 31
Joshua Howland (10) 32
Maximilian Thorpe (10) 33
Lewis King (11) 34
James Wood (10) 35
Megan Hobbs (11) 36
Joe Giles (11) 36
Freddy Allen (10) 37
Joshua Cumming-Webb (10) 37
Scarlett Howe (10) 38
Katherine Hutchinson (10) 38
Finn Bergstrom (10) 39
Cormac Flanagan (10) 39
Elish May Burney (11) 40

Lunsford Primary School, Aylesford

- Charlotte Thrower (11) 40
- Luke Clare (9) 41
- Laura Smith (10) 42
- Benjamin Baker (7) 42
- Kira Michel (11) 43
- George Baker (7) 43
- Ryan Smith (10) 44
- Ashleigh Osborne (11) 44
- Rebecca Hammond (10) 45
- Brandon-Lee Barker (8) 45
- Abbey Dearden (10) 46
- Chloe Banfield (10) 46
- Kelsey Rice (11) 47
- Ben Simkins (9) 47
- Ben Smith (11) 48
- Samantha Blue Nelson (9) 48
- Brandon Bennett-Stewart (10) 49
- Rianna Cripps (9) 49
- Ashleigh Alderman (10) 50
- William Handy (9) 50
- Jack Hyslop (11) 51
- Jasmine Smith (10) 51
- Samuel Jacob Smale (10) 52
- William Hellmuth (11) 52
- Ellie Rebecca King (9) 53
- Thomas M'Grady (10) 53
- Rhiannon Morgan (8) 54
- Rebecca Lynne Jaffray (11) 54
- Ryan Corcoran (11) 55
- Sebrena Hough (8) 55
- Mia Toni Atkin (9) 56
- Brooke Amschwand (9) 56
- Kieran Smith (8) 57
- Dalton Stone (8) 57
- Tinu Elejogun (8) 57
- Luisa Tebbutt (8) 58
- Kirsty Taylor (7) 58
- Sophie Smith (8) 58
- Matthew Sandwell (9) 59
- Molly Baker (9) 59
- Luke Simkins (7) 59
- Jessica Taylor (9) 60
- Isobel Jury-Sofi (8) 60
- Erin Haywood (7) 60
- Joshua Espadas (11) 61
- Jessica Lusher (10) 61
- Hope Emily Broadmore (9) 61
- Reese Aaron Saunders (9) 62
- Connor Matthew Evans (10) 62
- Rohan Smith (8) 62
- Katie Hardy (11) 63
- Callum Morgan (11) 63
- Ailsa Hellmuth (8) 63
- Layne Scott (7) 64
- Brody King (7) 64
- Emily Dearden (8) 64
- Tyler Dewhurst (8) 65
- James Bryer (7) 65
- Lucy Shaw (8) 65
- Sophie Colyer (10) 66

Our Lady's CP School, Dartford

- Niamh Jones (9) 66
- Olumide Babatunde (9) 67
- Caitlin Sims (9) 67
- Adeola Amao (8) 68
- Lauren Miller (9) 68
- Elizabeth Williams (9) 69
- Alice Goodwin (9) 69
- Daniel Luton (9) 70
- Jack Jukes (8) 70
- Fintan Cadden (8) 71
- Hulya Yosma (9) 71
- Mia Ridzwan (9) 71
- Dean Gonzales (9) 72
- Emily Jeeves (9) 72
- Joshua Ise (9) 72
- Sophie Glandfield (9) 73
- Seán Ryan (8) 73
- Sarah Johnson (8) 73
- Ellie Atkins (9) 74
- Evan Page (8) 74
- Megan Draper (8) 74

Alexandra Lynn (9) 75
Alex Ojo (8) 75

Riverside Primary School, Rainham

Rhys Branch (8) 75
Olivia May Bridges (8) 76
Lucie Stewart (8) 76
Elisse Smith (8) 77
Megan Wells (8) 77
Jade Schopman (9) 78
Samantha O'Rourke (7) 78
Lauryn Lelo (7) 79
Sophie Clarkson (7) 79
Harley Burr (8) 80
Lucy Cordier (7) 80
Nikita Skirth (7) 81
Melissa Godden (9) 81
Conor Murdoch (8) 82
Ryan Gordon (9) 82
Lauryn Hughes (7) 82
Stanley McQueen (8) 83
Chloe Tilley (7) 83
Alfie Plumb (7) 83
Sinead Brown (8) 84
Elysia Bradley (7) 84
William Scales (7) 84
Marco Aicolino (8) 85
Tommy Hambrook (8) 85
Danielle Pymm (7) 85
Ellie Reeder (8) 86
Jack Briggs (7) 86
Kieran Mallion (8) 86
Conor Sullivan (7) 87
Chloe-Jai Fendick (8) 87
Charlotte O'Rourke (9) 87
Shane Treeby (8) 88
William Gardner (8) 88
Joanne Keating (8) 88
Thalia Burr (7) 89
Leah Mai Harrison (8) 89
Beau Hall 89

Rosherville CE Primary School, Gravesend

Josh Saar (11) 90
Yasmine Burrha (10) 91
Vikki Smith (9) 91
Jamie-Leigh Yardley (11) 92
Emily Jane Ringer (9) 92
Tegan Rai (9) 93

St William of Perth School, Rochester

Keeley Stocker (11) 93
Amy Abbotson (11) 94
Heather McMahon (10) 94
Charlotte Byrne (11) 95
Eve Rushforth (11) 95
Sarah Louise Ireland (10) 96
Rachel Narborough (10) 96
Francesca Knight (11) 97
Katherine Knight (11) 97
John Paul Swain (10) 98
Libby Godfrey (10) 98
Michael Polley (11) 99
Cameron Payas (10) 99
Jack Waller (10) 100
Stephen McSwiney (10) 100
Joseph Smith (10) 101
Georgina Wolski (10) 101
Abbi De La Hoyde (10) 101
Mitchell Ekundayo Elba (10) 102

Stone St Mary's School, Greenhithe

Nicola Freer 102
Liam Massey 103
Ellenor Palmer (9) 104
Glenys Adelusi 105
Jordan Card (9) 105
Courtney Price (10) 106
Josh Lewis (9) 106
Ciaran Jones 107
Mylim Taylor-Gray (9) 107
Jack Coburn (10) 108

Gregory Hassall (9) 108
Corina Fox 109
Chloe Newton (10) 109
Chloe Lawrence (9) 110
Robyn King (9) 110
Grace Johnson 111
Toby Hooker (10) 111
Jordan Burgess 112
James Harding (10) 112
Cameron Rose (10) 113
Narayan Chatha (9) 113
Matthew Jones (10) 114
Liam Reed (10) 114
Amy Manchester (9) 114

Whitfield & Aspen School, Dover

Rebecca Artemis Preston (11) 115
Abbey Roberts (11) 115
Thrishali Sumanasekera (10) 116
Tom Wood (10) 116
Benjamin Kieran Harris (11) 117
Carl Hermon (10) 117
Chloe Burr (11) 118
Toby Clayton (10) 118
Callum Tanton (9) 119
Lewis Bird (9) 119
Jaimee Baldwin (10) 120
Beth Roberts (10) 120
Georgia Finnis (11) 121
Elisabeth Hall (10) 121
Amelia Ward (10) 122
Daniel Marshall (11) 122
Melodie Letchford (10) 123
Brendan Foottit (10) 123
Samuel Edwards (10) 124
Jasmine Graham (9) 124
Alex Riley (10) 125
Danielle Cole (11) 125
Ashley Baldwin (11) 126
Robyn Davison (11) 126
Dylan Proudlock-Damms (10) 127
Josh Fagg (11) 127
Gaby Northcott (11) 128

William Okou (11) 128
Jordan Bale (11) 129
Thomas Nunn (10) 129
Matthew Ashbee (9) 130
Amy Kansy (10) 130
Thomas Ashbee (11) 131
Alice Payne (10) 131
Hannah Gumbley (10) 132
Georgina Edmonds (11) 132
Jessie Smissen (10) 133
Aaron Edward Langley (10) 133
Ellie Tomkinson (9) 134
Bethany Whitehead (9) 134
Philip O'Flaherty (10) 135
Aimee Martin (9) 135
Leigha Mills (11) 136

The Poems

Poetry Explorers – Kent

Sweet Robin Redbreast

Wearing his scarlet coat as always
The robin hops along.
Holding his dagger-beak in the air
Singing his little song.

Dancing in the pale clouded sky
Does sweet robin redbreast
Hurry, hurry! Quick dearest friend
Quickly create your nest.

Keep your body warm through the cold months
With feathers, twigs and moss.
Finish your home as quick as you can
Or you will be at loss.

Now the chilly winter has started
Your hard work has paid off.
You can snuggle down lovely and warm
Without the slightest cough.

Well done sweet robin redbreast my friend,
As you have done quite well.
You have survived the first winter
But many more will come.

Molly Bradley (10)
Chiddingstone Primary School, Edenbridge

Little Robin

Little robin
A chilly nippy evening awakes
Poor little robin gently shakes
Fly little robin, fly to your nest
For there you may nap, sleep and rest.

A crimson shawl, a scarlet feathered vest
Cuddled up wonderfully warm, chirping merrily
Settling in to a twiggy winter nest
Matchstick legs, gripped feet rest
As dusk approaches
His outstretched wings
Wrap around the little robin's
Red crested breast.

Little robin, jolly and merry, silently sings
As the saffron sun sinks down yet lower
Therefore little robin must gently lay his head
Shut his beady raisin eyes
And sleep until morning does arise.

Louise Roche (11)
Chiddingstone Primary School, Edenbridge

Robin Redbreast

Robin, robin redbreast
In his feather red vest
Hurrying to make his twig nest
Never pausing to take a quick rest.

Robin, robin redbreast
Hurrying in a trance
Dagger at the ready
In case an enemy might prance.

Robin, robin redbreast
Acting very strong
Hopping along the branch
Singing a little song.

Robin, robin redbreast
His beak like a splinter
Sometimes I wonder
Will he survive this winter?

Ellalute Shamwana (10)
Chiddingstone Primary School, Edenbridge

Robin I Can See You!

The robin lands in a trance
The grass sways like an ocean dance.
The dagger pressed upon the frost bitten earth,
A December morning, it's the delicate first.
But the robin lives all winter
Swooping elegantly from each ghostly tree
To the clear ice blue sky, so free.

Claws like cutlasses although they're minute
But the top half is fragile like a small tranquil flute.
Little outstretched wings flutter frantically out
And a cat stalks ready to pounce.
Rejoice, robin's got away
He is going to live another day.
But his days are numbered each one becomes harder
And his scarlet scarf tightens, choking his neck to his death in his brittle nest!

Sophie Tyrrell (11)
Chiddingstone Primary School, Edenbridge

Poetry Explorers – Kent

Eagle

He soars through the field grasping his prey with his stiff crooked hands.
His tail swings in the wind like a Victorian petticoat.
He hunts his prey like a stalker.
His beak pointing forward like a cutlass.
His aggressive personality as he swoops down for the harmless mouse.
He sits on the mountain top, his arms an outstretched plane.
His beady eyes cannot be moved, they lock their target like a dart.
You cannot escape him, he will rip you limb by limb.
He plummets down to Earth, a rocket in flight.
A wool hat on his head.
His feathers the tip of an iceberg.
No one sees him as he approaches, they carry on with further notice.
He sees his tasty meal then goes in for the steal.

Tom Wiles (10)
Chiddingstone Primary School, Edenbridge

Eagle

An eagle is gliding through the air
No animal can escape its glare.
Claws as sharp as knives
They are the decider of death or life.
A killer in the air with a crooked beak
Food is what he seeks.
A movement is all it takes
His petticoat tail
Its wings like a sail.
A white balaclava covers his head
His eyes as deep as lead.
He is the lord of the sky
Death comes anywhere, even up high.

Jack Price (10)
Chiddingstone Primary School, Edenbridge

Little Robin

Christmas is calling and the robins are near
The return of the robin finally appears,
Nights are getting colder and he's on his own
Nowhere to sleep, nowhere to hide
The chance of being killed is by his side.
So hurry, hurry, go build your nest
Oh sweet little robin go and rest.
Dancing merrily he hops around
Twitches his head but no sound,
I love you red robin all jolly and red
Now fly away, fly away my dearest friend.

Melissa Harper (10)
Chiddingstone Primary School, Edenbridge

The Eagle

Swooping down with outstretched arms
Her snowy fan spread out behind.
She spots food crawling down below
A cunning plan forms on her mind.
She soars like lightning through the air
Her witch's fingers ready to strike
She sinks her bony nails in
As it slowly turns to night.
Tearing up her hopeless victim
With her cutlass crooked and long.
Oh eagle, how fierce you are
How proud and very strong.

Charlotte Crofts-Bolster (10)
Chiddingstone Primary School, Edenbridge

Fairies

Do you ever wonder
How nature gets its glow
And how the seasons come and go?
It's all the work of fairies
As they stay well out of sight
Every day and night.
When the first baby laughs
A fairy takes its flight,
All the way to the second star
And across the waves and
Lands at Pixie Hollow.

Anna Pullen (8)
Eastry CE Primary School, Eastry

The Midnight Theatre

The moon is a shining spotlight
That brightens up the midnight theatre
To make way for the dazzling sun
Radiant and gleaming
With its smooth, clean light.

Amy Sampson (9)
Eastry CE Primary School, Eastry

Go And Look Out The Window

(Inspired by 'Go and Open the Door' by Miroslav Holub)

Go and look out the school window
Maybe outside there's a big climbing wall or a tiny castle,
A hedge of yellow flowers or a mermaid,
Some stairs with five steps or a hot ocean,
Little children or a gigantic pony.
Go and look out the school window,
Maybe you'll see a horse or a magical horse.

Lucy Rafferty (8)
Eastry CE Primary School, Eastry

Imagine

Imagine a cat
As wide as a mat.
Imagine a gorilla
As tall as a pillar.
Imagine a bat
As big as a cat.
Imagine a bear
As big as a lair.
Imagine a grape
As long as tape.
Imagine a gown
As big as a town
And a clock the same size as a flock!

Ellie Coupland (8)
Eastry CE Primary School, Eastry

Bonfire Night

Fireworks whizzing in the sky
Sparklers waiting in the night
Lovely barbecue cooking food for us to eat
This is a time we all have some fun.

Fireworks zoom in the sky
Sizzling and crackling way up high
We all think it's interesting
That's why we all come
Whoa!

Henry Armstrong (8)
Eastry CE Primary School, Eastry

Bonfire Night

F ireworks up in the sky
I look right up so high
R acing, the Catherine wheel goes by
E ating popcorn while they go
W hizzing fireworks going so high and people going, 'Whoa!'
O n November fifth there are popping bangers
R unning to watch the fireworks
K eeping the children away from the rockets
S werving up and down.

Sam Cott (8)
Eastry CE Primary School, Eastry

Quickly

Quickly the cheetah runs on the plain,
Quickly the mill turns wheat into grain.
Quickly the penguins jump, swim and dive
Quickly the bees fly out of the hive.

Quickly the sun gets chased away by the night,
Quickly the argument turns into a fight.
Quick is the hare but quickest of all
Is the water rushing over the waterfall.

Becky Baker (9)
Eastry CE Primary School, Eastry

Loudly

Loudly the man started up the car,
Loudly he screamed when he dropped the jar.
Loudly the girl trod on her toe,
Loudly the boy did up his bow.

Loudly the boy cried for his mum
Loudly the girl shouted 'Please come'
Loud is the clap but loudest of all is
Humpty falling off the wall!

Alicia Prestleton (9)
Eastry CE Primary School, Eastry

Loudly

Loudly the boy sucked his thumb,
Loudly the friend shouted, 'Over here chum.'
Loudly the boy played away
Loudly the neighbour shouted, 'Hey!'

Loudly the woman revved her car,
Loudly the man strummed his guitar.
Loud is the gun but loudest of all
Is a boy being scrunched up in a ball.

James Ball (8)
Eastry CE Primary School, Eastry

Loudly

Loudly the children sang,
Loudly the fireworks went *bang!*
Loudly the boy shouted for Mum,
Loudly the man banged on the drum.

Loudly the dustbin van came up our road,
Loudly the boy shouted out the code.
Loud is the combine harvester cutting the corn
But loudest of all is the noise of the horn.

Emily Burton (9)
Eastry CE Primary School, Eastry

Winter Day

Chunks of snow avalanching off the roofs
Needly, bitter-cold snow carpeting
Northerly fierce winds blast breezes of snow
Beautiful snow glistens in the fresh smelling breezes
Sharp frosts attack like an army of soldiers
Wet, crackling snow crunches as excited children climb up the hills with their sleighs
The pattering of snow falling gets more exciting every time!
The graceful transparent snowflakes dance in the wind
Big snowman stands proud in the blizzard-like conditions
Ice blocks are as freezing as a freezer
Beautiful trees stand right in the centre of the amazing atmosphere
Water drips from branch to branch and then it freezes
The robin sings a cheerful happy tune.

Will Tumber (7)
Grove Park Community School, Sittingbourne

Bye-Bye

Bye-bye birds
Bye-bye trees
Bye-bye bugs
Bye-bye leaves.

Bye-bye our cabin
We're on our way home
Can't wait to see the rabbits
Or call Nanny on the phone.

Bye-bye our holiday
It's a shame to go
But soon we'll have another one
Just as fun, I know.

Mai Tumber (9)
Grove Park Community School, Sittingbourne

Easter Bunny

E aster eggs from the Easter bunny
A nimals are born
S pring flowers
T ulips and daisies
E veryone hunting for Easter eggs
R oses and sunflowers

B ring Easter eggs for an Easter party
U nderneath the flowers are tiny things
N ewborn chicks are hatching
N ewborn birds spread their wings
Y ellow flowers.

Emily Davis (9)
Grove Park Community School, Sittingbourne

Summer Holidays

On holiday is the place to be,
Drinking coffee and cold ice tea.
On the beach in the sun,
Playing and sunbathing, having fun.
Going to restaurants every night,
Dancing and singing on karaoke night.
Going to swimming pools, down the flumes,
Lying in the sun, singing tunes.

Olivia Holyoake (9)
Grove Park Community School, Sittingbourne

My Grandad

I love to walk with Grandad; his steps are slow like mine,
He doesn't say 'Hurry up', he always takes his time.
I love to walk with Grandad; his eyes see things like mine.
Most people just push and shove and don't stop to see
I'm so glad that God made Grandad unrushed and almost as young as me.
I'm extremely proud to call you my grandad and you mean the whole world to me.

Charlotte Quinn (8)
Grove Park Community School, Sittingbourne

Birthday

B irthdays are a time for giving
I n houses they give parties
R eligious celebrations
T iny people's birthdays are really fun
H aving presents if lots of fun
D ays are fun when it's your birthday
A bsolutely amazing
Y ellow, red and pink parcels around.

Eloisa Walsom (9)
Grove Park Community School, Sittingbourne

Boggis, Bunce And Bean

Boggis, Bunce and Bean are a bunch of bumbling bees
Bumping and banging, bumbling balls eager to kill
Bunce is a small dwarf, bumping and bumbling
Boggis is as tall and as fat as a pig in his mitt
Bean on the other hand, is eager to drink more cider
But when he drinks too much, he turns against his friends to kill!

Joe Matten (8)
Grove Park Community School, Sittingbourne

Stars

S ee the midnight blue sky with small sparkling figures
T winkling stars fill the sky with joy and happiness
A marvellous sight to see and enjoy
R avishing lights as bright as the sun
S parkling stars in the moonlight sky, oh so magnificent.

Tara Winterbourn (9)
Grove Park Community School, Sittingbourne

Snow

S now is as pretty as a princess
N obody hates snow, it's great
O h, how great is the snow
W henever it's going to stop I don't care, I'm just glad it's here!

Cerys Demomme (9)
Grove Park Community School, Sittingbourne

The Night Before Christmas

The night before Christmas
The children sleeping in their lovely cosy beds
None of them know what story lies ahead of their lovely dreams!

Renee Quartey-Peluola (8)
Grove Park Community School, Sittingbourne

Along The Empty Desert Sand

Along the empty desert land
Behold, a peachy pale sand
The wind that blows
The sun that glimmers
Along the line of sand that shimmers.

The camels that travel
The people who wander
To see the pyramids beyond yonder
Everyone chats
While wearing beach hats
Along the empty desert land.

On the sand there people lay
Enjoy the view, come today
Unfortunately your time has ended
But has your day been splendid
Along the empty desert land?

Jade Warner (11) & Hannah Batchelor (10)
Long Mead CP School, Tonbridge

What Is Red?

Red is the crackle of an evil witch
The mean voice of a snitch
A warm sunset
Juicy strawberries in a bowl
A red hot chilli
Screams of pain
Love bonding in an alley
A field of poppies in a valley
A bride's bouquet
Blossom on the trees in May
Slices of melon
Fruit salads
Freshly picked cranberries
A blood-filled battleground
Flaming torch lights in the dungeons
The scream of fright as the Devil appears
The call of a parrot looking for a mate
A robin's breast
Carnations in a vase
Pomegranates in a bowl
The roar of a fearless dragon
The blood of a ran-over fox.

Ellie Turner (10)
Luddenham School, Faversham

Untitled

My spirits sink like a scuppered ship submerged in the ink-black sea
I sink into the shadows waiting for you to go away
I fall like a wounded animal blood seeping from my heart
Sitting like a condemned man slumped, waiting for my fate
Like a stranded child walled up behind a ravine of sorrow and anger.

When . . .
I am like a man being taken to prison solemnly watching the horizon
I see faces masked with a picture of contempt
See souls showing nothing but hostility
Lost in a land of sorrow and misery my mind filled with anguish
I hate myself everything around me.

You . .
Screaming but without a noise
My face burns, my eyes sting
I wander in a world of evil humiliation
Meandering through Hell
The boiling blood beats a wild rhythm in my head
I stand and fall, stand, fall, stand and fall until I find the courage to stay standing.

When you bully me!

Frank Radcliffe-Adams (10)
Luddenham School, Faversham

Night Creeps

The night swallows me whole,
A dark blanket covering the Earth.
The swings in the abandoned park
Slowly swinging as if someone was sitting there that I could not see.
The bare trees reaching for me as if they are alive.
Stars are sparkling, the mist is creeping,
Something strange is going on.
Lamp post light looking terribly scary at night.
There are green eyes staring at me,
Watching, talking, planning an attack.
I hope this is just a dream.

The moonlight overpowering all in the sky
Black creatures swooping like a bird for its prey,
Nothing can get in his way.
The grass crunching under whose or what feet.
I am sure it would be something I would not like to meet!
Even though I am tucked up at home
It feels like I'm all alone.
Black shadows coming for me
Please, oh please, be a dream.

Hazel-Anne Frost (10)
Luddenham School, Faversham

Back Street Boozer

Dark shadows creeping close into the brick
Bolted doors like jail bars
Gloomy lamp posts
Screams haunting the background
Bodies lying on the floor like a black cat hunting
Looking into windows you see shadows arguing
Lurching dustbins
Dogs barking like drums booming
Flags littering the floor.

Bats swooping so low you could touch them
Party hats, last night's dance
Smashed holes as someone was trying to get out
Pools of blood dripping from spikes on alley rails
Bottles smashed
Crashed motorbikes with oil flooding the ground
Gurgling drains
A feel of cold like a ghost touching you
Footsteps creeping in the darkness.

Angus Clarke (10)
Luddenham School, Faversham

Bully, Bully Over There

I hide in my shell like a pearl in an oyster
My eyes pour with water from the chlorine in the pool
I feel like a piece of dirt from the magical underground pit
And my lips are so sore from the heat of the sun.

When . . .
I suffer from the pain coming from my toes up to my head
My ears sting from the kids shouting at me all day long
When you make me clean your room you are torturing me
I am as worthless as a can being thrown into a bin.

You . . .
My tummy churns as if I am riding the biggest roller coaster
                                                in the world
I feel like a flower without any bloom.
And a snowman, with no carrot for a nose
I am a leaf but without any green
My cheeky cheeks bloom from embarrassment.

Bully me!

Christina Kenton (10)
Luddenham School, Faversham

Night In The Street

From up in my bedroom window
I can see the murky dark grey street
Where stray animals run around
Whispering beneath my feet.

From up in my bedroom window
People shout and scream
With their dogs yapping beside them
Licking their great jaws clean.

From up in my bedroom window
Lamp posts flicker in the light
Whilst the trees sing a scary tune
All about the deep dark night.

From up in my bedroom window
The subway rattles past
With all the things making noise around me
I wonder when night will last.

Robyn Hilliard (10)
Luddenham School, Faversham

Bully!

I feel like a lost child wandering in unknown territories
Like a pilot jumping out of a spitfire whose parachute is jammed
You treat me as if I am a dead fox on the roadside
And I am a condemned man seeing the happy moments of his life,
                                                      before the electric chair.

When . . .
You are the ghosts in my nightmares
And I am a fire with no heat
A book with blank pages
And the school with no pupils.

You . . .
My mind is a dark whirlpool
A car with no engine
The injured wolf cub, not accepted anywhere
My heart will rot away if you keep on bullying me.

Bully me!

Daniel Klein (10)
Luddenham School, Faversham

Night At The River

Bats hiding in the trees
A surface of land for foxes to run
Bushes blowing in the cold wind
The shimmering moon reflecting into the river.

Rats scattering down the side
Silent sleeping all around me
Owls hooting calm and quietly
Grass swishing in the breeze.

Everything still but only slightly
Cars passing by from time to time
The pitch-black sky shining over
Making almost everything unseen.

The river drifting passing peacefully
Shadows creeping up behind you
Not one person in sight
But there might be something in the woods . . .

Grace McGrath (10)
Luddenham School, Faversham

Night At An Abandoned Station

Outside is full of creatures and blackness,
Loud screams and black stillness
The sound of robbers fills the black
Rats jump, track to track,
The whistle from a cold icy night.

Night is made of three different things
Sometimes it can be friendly, more fright,
The third thing is history
Cats watching in the dark
Broken trains being vandalised by Death himself
And broken wood snake.

Ghost trains rule the area
Ticket machines shaking mysteriously
Tripped up tickets blowing in the misty gloom
Time slipping . . .
Dawn coming.

Harry Elliott Taylor (10)
Luddenham School, Faversham

Bully!

My stomach whizzes around like a Catherine wheel
I feel like a firework waiting to explode
My heart falls apart like a cracker being pulled
And I'm as sad as a puppy lost in the snow.

When . . .
My tears fall like a waterfall
I hide in my shell like a tortoise
A lion without its mane
And a flower without any petals.

You . . .
I feel like a pheasant flying away from a gunshot
I'm as worthless as the rubbish in the bin
My tears are as cold as ice
And I'm as sad as a fox cub being away from its mother.

Bully me!

Paige Sheaff (10)
Luddenham School, Faversham

When You Bully Me...

I feel like a fox that has lost its cubs
A plane that has no engine
The world without any people
I hide in my shell like I have no face

When...
I am the only star that has lost its light
A friendless person
A mirror without a reflection
A dragon without any fire

You...
I am a leopard that has lost its spots
A tree without any leaves
A bed without any mattress
My eyes cry tears like a rock cave.

Bully me...

Lilly-May Pilcher (11)
Luddenham School, Faversham

When You Bully Me . . .

I hide in my shell like my face has never shown
My heart sinking like the Titanic
I am worthless like the rubbish bin
And I cry tears that I've never shown.

When . . .
I am the only star that has lost its glimmer
I am a bottle you shake, waiting to explode
A tiger without its stripes
And my eyes look like burning coals on a roasting fire.

You . . .
I am a flower without any petals
I feel like a book with no pages
I'm a mirror which has just been cracked
And I'm like the world without any people.

Bully me!

Jessica Childs (11)
Luddenham School, Faversham

Bully, Bully

I cry like someone has broken me
My tears are like a waterfall
I am a star that has no shine
And I'm a tree with no leaves.

When
I am like a book with no pages
I am worthless as rubbish in the bin
I am a fire with no coal
And my heart melts like ice cream.

You
I hide in my shell like a tortoise
My eyes are red and sore
I will be a flower who has lost its bloom
And a kitten without its ball of string.

Bully me.

Poppy Johnson (10)
Luddenham School, Faversham

Bully!

My head keeps banging like a firework
My tummy turns over like a roller coaster
I'm nothing, like a rainbow with no colour
And I cry tears like a waterfall.

When . . .
My red hot heart is louder than a drum in a rock band
My eyes are like a lost star with no light
I'm a butterfly that keeps flying away and a snail hiding in a shell.

You . . .
A tiger without stripes
Apple crumble without the crumble
The diamond without its sparkle
And the trees without blossom in summer.

Bully me!

Abbie Ramsden (10)
Luddenham School, Faversham

If Pebbles Could Speak

I am unique you will never find my matching pair.
You can find me all around the world.
I may hold something fossilised preserved of millions of years.
You crush me underneath your shoes but you never know I'm there.
My home is upon the seabed where I rest until washed shore.
You use me like a spotted carpet stretched for miles along the shore.
Once you throw me in the sea, I am lost forever.
The only thing I ever hear is the roll of breaking waves.
I come in many shapes and sizes.

Emily Carter (10)
Luddenham School, Faversham

Night

Silence steals the night away
Nightingales scared to sing
Shadows creeping through the darkness
Cats are screeching
And glass is smashing.
Night reveals itself tonight
Pine cones falling mysteriously
Eyes wandering everywhere like cameras
Only star-gazers know the dark
Windmills spinning
And charms clashing.
The moon shines like never before
Bats hanging on for dear life
Broken up benches, bins and cartwheels
And robbers casing the joint.

Joshua Howland (10)
Luddenham School, Faversham

Poetry Explorers – Kent

If Pebbles Could Speak

I know I'm unique, there's nothing quite like me,
I'm used as a carpet but am picked up and chucked.
Buried forever for you to enjoy the summer.
I trap dead insects and show the skeletons
It takes some thousands of years to come.
I'm precious to you when picked up and polished
Smooth or sharp, worn down by the sea.
Why do you toss and chuck me about?
You think I'm lifeless, no feelings at all,
How did I come here? Answer that!
I know lots of secrets, bad and good as I listen to all of you,
I know how you speak and how you think.
I get thrown into the sea and don't come back.
Sitting all day with nothing to do
Just being disturbed by children, listening to you!

Maximilian Thorpe (10)
Luddenham School, Faversham

What Is Black?

Black is ghosts in graveyards ripping souls
Shadows lurking around the corner
Palm trees swaying from side to side in the hurricane
Owls tweeting in dark nights
Black is whipped chocolate ice cream
A lump of coal
South Americans digging in mines
It's nightmares
Gutters breaking out with rats and mud
Black is Hallowe'en in deep, creepy thoughts
Vampires sucking blood
Black is a paintbrush, brushing on sugar paper
Covered in mud at a Sunday football game
Zombies walking down alleys
Witches flying on broomsticks.

Lewis King (11)
Luddenham School, Faversham

Night From My Window

Shadows sneaking round the garages
The lamp posts shining but not the right colour
Cars starting with no one starting them
Outside a whistle in the wind
Post boxes speaking like humans
Ticket machine walking mysteriously
Trees walking to the shop near Boots
Recycle bins spitting out glass
Fish and chips wrappers rustling down the road
Spotlights looking for cats on the side of the road
Bins clanking in the middle of darkness
Bats flapping in full darkness
Back doors slamming like smashing windows
Cats rowing with dogs in gardens
Roads lifting like a human jumping.

James Wood (10)
Luddenham School, Faversham

View From A Hotel Window

Silently the sparkling stars watch over us all night long
The frozen lake glistens in the light of the moon
While the trees sway in the light breeze
The deserted park sleeps and dreams of the next day.

The sleepy cats wander around the frozen lake
The moon shines over the valleys below
All you can hear are trains running along the bumpy tracks
Snowy mountains above everything watching over everyone
                                            to keep them safe.

Silently the sparkling stars watch over us all night long
People's houses silent, not even a mouse could be heard
Morning is coming closer
Night is fading away.

Megan Hobbs (11)
Luddenham School, Faversham

If Pebbles Could Speak

I'm as smooth as silk
You can throw me away but I'll come back another day
I can be an uncomfortable chair
You stand on me when you're walking
Sometimes you trip on me when you walk along the road
I can come in different colours
I hear the tides turn for thousands of years
Sometimes the sea makes me sparkle
You have me around a fire
The sea washes me around.

Joe Giles (11)
Luddenham School, Faversham

If Pebbles Could Speak

You call me one but there are millions of me.
I'm a smooth carpet, you see me everywhere.
I'm sharp, I'm smooth, I'm shiny and fly in my game.
I'm buried everywhere you stand and you hurt me with every step.
I can be small, big, massive, tiny, colourful and shiny.
You find me here and there, but mostly at sea.
I'm round and get chucked by you, but why?
I lie and don't move unless you touch me.
You kick me and leave me all alone why?
I hide and stay where I am and listen to every word you say.
I have holes or cracks in me but you take no notice.
You think I have no feelings, no face no nothing.
But really I am a lot more that you think, I have feelings and a face.

Freddy Allen (10)
Luddenham School, Faversham

Mist On The Wharf

Mist seeps through cracks and keyholes
Boats creak and groan
Cats jump from roof to mast to boat
The scavenger scours for fish and mice
And shouts go up of midnight mooring.

Smuggler unload this week's contraband
Through mist and fog on trap and cart
The moon's aura shows through the ghostly clouds
The lamp's flames flicker and die
Night takes all those still awake to slumber and then to wake.
Dawn looms in dark corners, ready to light the new day.

Joshua Cumming-Webb (10)
Luddenham School, Faversham

Walking With The Night

When the sun goes down night goes for a walk around the town.
The lonely swings creak in the regular gusts of wind,
Small, large, all sizes of footsteps walk up and down the alley,
Locks turning, forest burning,
Door handles open when its owner goes for a fun night out.
Foxes and rats battle for the remains of the dustbins,
Street lamps glow a pale lemon light.
In the early hours of morning, the clanking of the bottles wake the
restless sleepers
Though the milkmen are trying to be as quiet as feet landing on the
soft summer sand
Owls hooting, morning walking to overtake the long walk of night.

Scarlett Howe (10)
Luddenham School, Faversham

Dead Lake

Shadows wander over the broken barge
But there is no one except people of the past
Who go near the water wasteland.
It is black, even in the sunlight.
It is frozen during the summer and it is misty through the
clearest of days.
The rusted railing haunts every eye which has seen it rumble
Bit by bit tear by tear into the gloom below.
Whispers which have gathered all of them have come and gone
But yet all of them are still being spoken on the lips of the wind
And are being heard by the ears of the leaves.
That is the life of the dead lake.

Katherine Hutchinson (10)
Luddenham School, Faversham

What Is Black?

Black is still darkness outside
Coal on the fire crackling in the heat
The rainbow taken by the shadow
A maggot writhing on a hook
Old engine oil on a page of a book
The sound of twigs cracking underfoot

A black hole roaring ever nearer, *beware!*
The feeling of a ghost creeping up on you
A nightmare I cannot escape from
Forever falling
Smoke floating in the air.

Finn Bergstrom (10)
Luddenham School, Faversham

If Pebbles Could Speak

You stand on me while you walk to the sea
I am thrown into a sea like an Olympic diver
There are lots of me but I can be unique
I am smooth but can be rough
I go in the sea but can't swim
I'm as smooth as a block of ice
A hopeless baby on the floor
They walk on me like a carpet
I can be many magical colours
I hurt if you are hit by me
I've heard the waves in the ocean.

Cormac Flanagan (10)
Luddenham School, Faversham

Night Street

Late at night, when you're asleep
Shadows creep,
Bins banging, owls hooting,
Cars revving, witches flying,
People dying.
Lights fading as morning dawns dawning
Ghosts gathering around the town square
Cameras scanning, red alert
Buses clashing in the wind
Phone boxes ring, no one there.

Elish May Burney (11)
Luddenham School, Faversham

The Other Side Of The Moon

The moon is strong
The moon is round
If it wasn't
It would fall to the ground.

You only see one half at tea
What happens on the other side is a mystery
There could be aliens
Who are oh so grand

With a throne
And pole in hand
Oh how he thinks he's oh so grand
The alien on the moon.

Charlotte Thrower (11)
Lunsford Primary School, Aylesford

Space

S is for space
O is for orbit
L is for light
A is for astronauts
R is for rockets

S is for stars
Y is for a year
S is for satellite
T is for an alien's tear
E is for Earth
M is of Mars

A is for atmosphere
N is for Neptune
D is of dangerous meteors

N is for NASA
E is for ET
P is for planets
T is for terrestrial
U is for Uranus
N is of night
E is for planet Earth.

Luke Clare (9)
Lunsford Primary School, Aylesford

The Other Side Of The Moon

The other side of the moon
Aliens play.
The little aliens cry all day,
The adult aliens mind their own business
Or maybe look after the alien children.

The other side of the moon
Aliens go on their trip to the park
Or maybe play hide in the dark.
Little aliens watch their mum cook
Before bed, little aliens read a book.

The other side of the moon
Bedtime is always a pain.
The adult aliens have to pull out the cane.
Aliens always have a way
Some aliens love to try to look at Earth all day.

The other side of the moon
That we can't see
We wonder what alien life could be.
We wonder what aliens do
But could aliens be true?

Laura Smith (10)
Lunsford Primary School, Aylesford

Ben

B en is a good boy
E very sum is easy
N ever naughty.

Benjamin Baker (7)
Lunsford Primary School, Aylesford

Alien Thief

Gooey, slimy, green, hairy,
He came into my room
He stole my ted
And took it away to the moon!

Gooey, slimy, green, hairy,
He came to the pool
He stole my rubber ring
And took it to the moon's shopping mall!

Gooey, slimy, green, hairy,
He came into the zoo
Going to take it to the moon
He stole my kangaroo!

Gooey, slimy, green, hairy,
He came into the sea
And away to the moon
Away to the far side of the moon
He went with me!

Kira Michel (11)
Lunsford Primary School, Aylesford

Acrostic Name Poem

G ood at numeracy
E very Saturday I go on my Wii
O n TV I watch 'Tom & Jerry'
R eally jumps a lot
G eorge is my name
E xcited about my new Wii game.

George Baker (7)
Lunsford Primary School, Aylesford

Aliens Like You

Sometimes I wonder what's on the other side of the moon
There could be aliens
With two heads,
One foot,
One toe,
Ten eyes,
Eight arms,
I hope I don't meet them soon!

But the aliens on the dark side of the moon
What would they think of you?
They might think you have
One eye,
Two tongues,
Nine tentacles,
Three feet,
Two mouths,
They won't want to meet us at noon!

Ryan Smith (10)
Lunsford Primary School, Aylesford

Moon

T he moon is full of scary monsters living on a bay
H e or she lies down all day
E ating slimy, gooey things

M unching away while watching Saturn's rings
O range, slimy, gooey things
O nly they can see, they're
N ot that different from me.

Ashleigh Osborne (11)
Lunsford Primary School, Aylesford

Dark Side Of The Moon

You see the moon
Up in the sky
You think you see it all
But that is a lie.

There is a side
Which no man can see
The darkest of all
Where nothing can be.

What's on that side?
No one knows
There could be aliens
Throwing shows.

I wish I could say
There, aliens cry
That is so sad
And it's a lie!

Rebecca Hammond (10)
Lunsford Primary School, Aylesford

Acrostic Name Poem

B randon is a good boy
R eally good at football
A good runner
N ever seen a ghost
D oes like a nap
O nly on Saturday I play football
N ice and kind.

Brandon-Lee Barker (8)
Lunsford Primary School, Aylesford

Are There Aliens On The Moon?

Are there aliens on the moon?
Who knows, do they sit down flat?
Are there aliens on the moon?
Who knows, do they wear hats?

Are there aliens on the moon?
Who knows, do they live in a house?
Are there aliens on the moon?
Who knows, would they eat a mouse?

Are there aliens on the moon?
Who knows, would they climb trees?
Are there aliens on the moon?
Who knows, do they have knees?

Well no, aliens do not live on the moon
But we will find out soon!

Abbey Dearden (10)
Lunsford Primary School, Aylesford

This Time I Will Be There

This time I will be there to see the rockets burst up into the sky
But will I be there to see them come back down?
I wish I could go up into space, wouldn't it be cool?
I would not even have to go to school.
I wish I could be like Neil Armstrong
But I would like to be the first one to step on Mars
And all I would be able to eat is chocolate bars.
I would like to discover life forms on Mars
But I don't like flying!

Chloe Banfield (10)
Lunsford Primary School, Aylesford

There Is Always A Side Of The Moon We Never See

There is always a side of the moon we never see
Sometimes I wonder what up there could be
I like to imagine there's a magical land
Maybe even something amazingly grand.

There's always a side of the moon we never see
Sometimes I wonder what life runs free
Maybe doves and magpies that flutter by
Or even talking trees, but that's a lie.

There is always a side of the moon we never see
Sometimes I wonder if that could be me
Dancing and prancing around on the moon
I wish I could go there so, so soon.

Kelsey Rice (11)
Lunsford Primary School, Aylesford

The Alien From Leeds

There was an alien from Leeds
Who bought a packet of seeds.
He planted them in the ground
And they were eaten up by his hand.

There was a small alien covered in fluff
He liked to think he was tough.
Food is what this alien likes
But he's not big enough to ride bikes.

Ben Simkins (9)
Lunsford Primary School, Aylesford

People Say: Beyond The Earth

Beyond the Earth (people say) there are many beauties to see
So when I look up at the sky at night I smile with glee
But the one thing that catches my eye is the moon that smiles at me.

The moon in the night sky looks like the size of a pie
But if ever I went to the moon I would say, 'Oh my!'

There is one part of the moon that is in complete dark
Who knows what's on the other side of the moon
There might be trees with bark or possibly aliens, animals or larks.

What about if possibly there was another me?
It seems to me that the moon shines all the time
But I know that one half doesn't.

Though there is one thing I do know
The one that shines the most is the one in you.

Ben Smith (11)
Lunsford Primary School, Aylesford

Alice The Alien

Alice the alien
Went to Mars
And wanted to see some stars.

Alice the alien
Went to Saturn
And a lot happened.

Alice the alien
Went to Mercury
And had some surgery.

Samantha Blue Nelson (9)
Lunsford Primary School, Aylesford

Poetry Explorers – Kent

The Spectacular Moon

The man has been to the moon
But not the other side
If he sees something scary
He will have to go and hide.

The moon is round and white
And people think it is bright
I think it's not
They must have forgot.

The moon is very small
And it will never fall
If you go and see the moon
It is as big as a hall.

Brandon Bennett-Stewart (10)
Lunsford Primary School, Aylesford

Solar System

S tars like suns shimmer brightly in the night
O ther planets whizzing round
L ittle aliens running wild on Mars
A nother life form forming on Mars
R ockets shooting into outer space.

S aturn's rings moving quickly
Y oung astronauts visit the moon
S un's rays hit the Earth
T iny rocks hit the planets
E arth's moon orbiting in space
M eteors crash into Saturn and Jupiter.

Rianna Cripps (9)
Lunsford Primary School, Aylesford

Space

Space is exciting with Neptune and Mars
Don't forget Uranus, the moon and stars.
There is also Mercury, Venus and the Earth
If the Earth was flat I would definitely surf.

Jupiter and Saturn are much, much greater
Quick, turn the rocket, before we hit a crater.
Mars has lots of burning mountains
To make it cool down it should have a fountain.

The sun is hot like a teapot
The moon is cool like a frozen swimming pool.
Pluto's not actually a planet
Even though my name's not Janet.

Ashleigh Alderman (10)
Lunsford Primary School, Aylesford

I Did A Race

I went to space
I did a race
I didn't win
So I got thrown in the bin!
I took off my shoes
I couldn't choose
An alien called Bob
With a big job
An alien called Rob
With a big gob
To coach me!

William Handy (9)
Lunsford Primary School, Aylesford

Poetry Explorers – Kent

Wicked Moon!

Far away, out in space
There is a place
That everyone can see
It's good for you and good for me.

Waxing and waning in the midnight sky
Astronauts relaxing, eating a pie
Armstrong lands at dusk
Nothing to do with elephant tusks.

The moon, the moon, it is so bright
Nothing to do but reflecting light
It can only reflect one half
So follow its magical path.

Jack Hyslop (11)
Lunsford Primary School, Aylesford

What Am I?

I am a giant star, I have no rings and I am not blue.
You cannot drive to me in a car; it would take over two-hundred years.
I shine and light up your world, I am the biggest thing in the solar system.
The middle of me is very hot; the temperature is fifteen million centigrade.
My rays hit you in straight lines
My surface is about six-thousand centigrade and no one has ever explored me.
What am I?

Jasmine Smith (10)
Lunsford Primary School, Aylesford

Having An Alien For Tea

The North Star is a home to a tiny alien that loves pie.
The star is a glistening dragon's eye
When the alien awoke, he realised he felt down and blue.
He decided to call his best friend Bob
Who loved to gobble up stew.
He invited him round to play and eat
The tiny alien cooked ten pies and ten stews just for a treat,
His best friend, Bob, arrived in his new blue and orange rocket.
Luckily the tiny alien reminded him to lock it.
They played and danced and ran around all day
The time came to have tea, Bob saw he had stew he cried out
'Whohay!

Samuel Jacob Smale (10)
Lunsford Primary School, Aylesford

The Other Side Of The Moon

On the other side of the moon
There is a fat priest who sits in gloom.
On the other side of the moon
There is a mouse wearing Uggs and a tutu.
On the other side of the moon
There is a cow with designer hooves.
On the other side of the moon
Sits Neil Armstrong being a goon.
On the other side of the moon
Sits a lonely woman looking for a groom.
On the other side of the moon
Sits no one, I'm being a buffoon!

William Hellmuth (11)
Lunsford Primary School, Aylesford

The Zodiac

Aries, the ram, intuitive and creative
Cancer, the crab, snappy and happy
Sagittarius, the hunter, caring and sharing
Taurus, the bull, strong and never wrong
Leo, the lion, tough not rough
Gemini, the twins, exciting and delighting
Virgo, the lady graceful and beautiful
Capricorn, the goat, charming, never harming
Pisces, the fish energetic, not pathetic
Aquarius, the sea, relaxed and laid-back
Scorpio, the scorpion, protective but affective
Libra, the scales, loyal and likes the royals.

Ellie Rebecca King (9)
Lunsford Primary School, Aylesford

The Dark Side Of The Moon

On the dark side of the moon
Creatures may lurk
On the dark side of the moon
Cities may exist.

Many of us believe in life
On the dark side of the moon
Aliens could be in hiding
On the dark side of the moon.

The dark side of the moon
Contains many, many secrets
Travel there you must to unravel my story.

Thomas M'Grady (10)
Lunsford Primary School, Aylesford

Acrostic Name Poem

R eally crazy
H ates too much chocolate
I s a drama queen
A lways late for school
N oisy sometimes
N ormally a bit naughty
O bviously clever
N ever had a detention in Year 3.

Rhiannon Morgan (8)
Lunsford Primary School, Aylesford

Moon

M any stars shine so bright, they fill the magical sky
                                        glowing magically
O ver we see the moon as we see one side, the other side
                                                never shows
O ver and over again dark moon turns but then again, we never
                                                  see that side
N o sign can I see, a mystery this must be.

Rebecca Lynne Jaffray (11)
Lunsford Primary School, Aylesford

What Is On The Other Side Of The Moon?

Many different things may live on the moon,
Dogs, cats or even a small goldfish
Over rocks, over craters anything could be there,
Living silently on the dark side of the moon
On the moon there are tiny blobs, orbiting the great moon,
Squelch, squelch little globalos live on the moon
Now you know what is on the moon.

Ryan Corcoran (11)
Lunsford Primary School, Aylesford

Acrostic Name Poem

S ebrena is my name
E very day I like to learn
B reena is my nickname
R uns like a snail
E ven when I don't like peas I eat them
N aughty Nancy is my cousin
A nimals are the best.

Sebrena Hough (8)
Lunsford Primary School, Aylesford

My Poem About Planets

P luto got sacked by the solar system
L aunch a rocket and if it goes too far please try and stop it
A strodome shows you all the planets and stars there are
N eptune shines and shimmers with its one blue ring
E arth goes round and round like a carousel
T rees and plants only grow on Earth
S tars glisten while making a pretty constellation.

Mia Toni Atkin (9)
Lunsford Primary School, Aylesford

Aliens

A liens are all green and slimy
L ots of aliens live in space
I n space you might see people
E ven though the aliens are slimy they are still very kind
N othing is pretty in space
S limy aliens that are very squeaky.

Brooke Amschwand (9)
Lunsford Primary School, Aylesford

Poetry Explorers – Kent

Acrostic Name Poem

K ind
I like pizza
E very week I play on my PS2
R eally kind
A good PS2 player
N ice boy.

Kieran Smith (8)
Lunsford Primary School, Aylesford

Acrostic Name Poem

D alton is kind and helpful
A nd I am good at launch pad
L ollipops are my favourite
T he book called 'Space Chimps' is my best book
O n Sunday I have a lay in
N ice and kind.

Dalton Stone (8)
Lunsford Primary School, Aylesford

Acrostic Name Poem

T rickster
I ndependent
N oisy
U sually untidy.

Tinu Elejogun (8)
Lunsford Primary School, Aylesford

Snow

I looked out of the flap and to my delight it was snowing.
I threw a snowball and it made a *zap!*
I woke up my sister, we ran down the stairs.
We went to the front garden and made a snowman
I used a carrot for its nose and buttons for a mouth.
This is the end of the snowy day.

Luisa Tebbutt (8)
Lunsford Primary School, Aylesford

Kirsty

K ind person
I like learning French on Fridays
R eally funny
S illy and crazy
T idy up carefully
Y es, I do love ice skating.

Kirsty Taylor (7)
Lunsford Primary School, Aylesford

Snowy Day

I looked out of my window, I smiled in surprise.
I ran outside to play in the wet snow and built a snowman.
I shivered some more, I was soaked to the skin.
What a nice day!

Sophie Smith (8)
Lunsford Primary School, Aylesford

Aliens

A liens all green and slimy
L iving on Mars all red and rusty
I n their flying saucer
E merald aliens jumping all around
N o aliens ever seen
S ome aliens are impossible to see.

Matthew Sandwell (9)
Lunsford Primary School, Aylesford

Space

The Milky Way is made of stars
A very red place is planet Mars.
Rings twirl round some of the planets
When the astronaut hits things he panics.
Round and round the black hole he goes,
Where he'll end up, nobody knows.

Molly Baker (9)
Lunsford Primary School, Aylesford

Acrostic Name Poem

L ucky and kind
U sing tools is what I enjoy
K icking balls is fun
E ating scampi is my favourite.

Luke Simkins (7)
Lunsford Primary School, Aylesford

Aliens

A liens are green
L iving here is very hard
I have a squishy face and squishy toes
E arth, you won't find me here
N either on Saturn
S pace is the best place.

Jessica Taylor (9)
Lunsford Primary School, Aylesford

Acrostic Name Poem

I am always untidy
S o good at sports day
O nly sometimes I am clumsy
B eautiful and clever as can be
E very weekend I practice my times tables
L ike me and be my friend.

Isobel Jury-Sofi (8)
Lunsford Primary School, Aylesford

Acrostic Name Poem

E very night at home, play a game called Rummikub
R eally good at skipping
I always go to ballet on Wednesday
N ice, kind, helpful.

Erin Haywood (7)
Lunsford Primary School, Aylesford

The Moon

Most people think there's no life on the moon
Some dull aliens might visit the moon
The moon is a dull place
So don't go to the moon
You'll get a huge travel bill!

Joshua Espadas (11)
Lunsford Primary School, Aylesford

Aliens Are Behind!

M any aliens live on the moon
O bserving the Earth with supersonic sight
O nly we cannot see that they live on the other side of the moon
N obody thinks that they are there but the moon is scattered
                                        with them everywhere.

Jessica Lusher (10)
Lunsford Primary School, Aylesford

Space Poem!

Rockets zooming into the air, fire coming out of the bottom
The planet Jupiter, orange and stripy
Aliens green, slimy and ugly
Living on planet Mars is great with aliens
Nobody believes in aliens.

Hope Emily Broadmore (9)
Lunsford Primary School, Aylesford

Space

S tars shining and glittering in the darkness
P lanets millions of miles away
A liens strange and mysterious
C omets zooming round Saturn
E arth, I'm glad to be home.

Reese Aaron Saunders (9)
Lunsford Primary School, Aylesford

Space

S hooting star whizzes across the atmosphere
P eople visited the moon and didn't know what to expect
A liens are green, ugly and slimy
C omets flying into Earth so fast you can only just see them
E veryone enjoys space.

Connor Matthew Evans (10)
Lunsford Primary School, Aylesford

Acrostic Name Poem

R ohan laughs all day
O nly read my Beano at bedtime
H appy all the time
A lways plays with my football
N ever tidy!

Rohan Smith (8)
Lunsford Primary School, Aylesford

The Mysterious Moon

M any moons are in the sky
O ne belongs to Earth
O ver one-hundred in the universe
N o one knows the exact number but neither you nor
                                       I will ever count them all!

Katie Hardy (11)
Lunsford Primary School, Aylesford

The Moon

M any people think that no life lives on the moon, but they're wrong
O range, green, blue too, aliens come in different colours
O val, square, circular too, aliens even come in the shape
                                            of balloons
N ot any human can ever know about these creatures.

Callum Morgan (11)
Lunsford Primary School, Aylesford

Acrostic Name Poem

A ilsa loves chocolate
I love my mum
L ikes doing drama
S o good at maths
A very nice girl.

Ailsa Hellmuth (8)
Lunsford Primary School, Aylesford

Acrostic Name Poem

L ovely and kind
A very bright girl
Y ou will want to be my friend
N ext week I am having a sleepover
E very day I watch TV.

Layne Scott (7)
Lunsford Primary School, Aylesford

Acrostic Name Poem

B ody fitness is good
R eally good runner
O n Monday I go to Beavers
D on't make me crazy
Y es, I eat chocolates.

Brody King (7)
Lunsford Primary School, Aylesford

Snowy Day

I looked out of my bedroom window, it was snowing.
I put warm clothes on and ran down the stairs.
I put my wellies on and went outside.
My brother hit me with a snowball, I was soaked.
Then I went inside, I was freezing.

Emily Dearden (8)
Lunsford Primary School, Aylesford

Acrostic Name Poem

T hinking all the time
Y es, I like pizza
L isten very carefully
E very day I brush my teeth twice
R unning is my favourite exercise.

Tyler Dewhurst (8)
Lunsford Primary School, Aylesford

Acrostic Name Poem

J ames is a good boy
A lways fast at running
M otorbikes are my favourite
E very night I go to bed when I'm told
S nakes are my favourite animals.

James Bryer (7)
Lunsford Primary School, Aylesford

Lucy

L ucy is my name
U sually playful
C areful thinker
Y esterday I went to Brownies.

Lucy Shaw (8)
Lunsford Primary School, Aylesford

The Moonlit Earth

M oonlit Earth
O n our planet it shines
O nly astronauts can land on the moon
N o one can see the other side.

Sophie Colyer (10)
Lunsford Primary School, Aylesford

Caitlin

Good friend
Share always
Loving forever
Food adorer
Pineapple lover
Pet carer
Always there
Loves snow
Good swimmer
Adores cake
Clever gymnast.

Niamh Jones (9)
Our Lady's CP School, Dartford

Cats

Mice catcher
Bird watcher
Lazy mover
Fish lover
Dog hater
Good licker
Bad scratcher
Greedy eater
Bad swimmer
Cosy cat.

Olumide Babatunde (9)
Our Lady's CP School, Dartford

My Mum

Always loving
My fan
Warm hugger
Big kisser
Cook hater
Very messy
Loud snorer
Loved one
Forever friend.

Caitlin Sims (9)
Our Lady's CP School, Dartford

The Sun

The sun is like a watermelon,
A golden slice in the sky.
It is like a parrot,
Colourful and bright.
The sun is like an orange,
Round, fat and juicy
It makes me want to eat it.
I know I cannot reach it.
The sun is like a burning fire, I love the sun.

Adeola Amao (8)
Our Lady's CP School, Dartford

My Birthday

My birthday is the 27th of November and I got a hat
On the hat there was a picture of a cat
I got a children's dictionary
As well as the game Pictionary.

I had my breakfast at the table
And on my chair there was a label
It said, 'Happy birthday Lauren'
Auntie Trish is coming today - she's foreign!

Lauren Miller (9)
Our Lady's CP School, Dartford

The Stars

The stars are shiny and bright
Heaven is lit up by the stars
Everybody loves the stars
Shining through the night
Together we stand and gaze at the stars
And the stars glisten down on us
Right now, right here,
Special friends, forever together.

Elizabeth Williams (9)
Our Lady's CP School, Dartford

The Circus

Funny fantasy
Jumping jokes
Acrobatic animals
Cunning candyfloss
Tense tightropes
Jinxing jugglers
The circus is great.

Alice Goodwin (9)
Our Lady's CP School, Dartford

The Sun

The sun is like a big, massive lightbulb
Shining on me
I think I'm going to melt
It's like I'm in an oven
I might be dinner
The sun is cooking me
Now I am turkey.

Daniel Luton (9)
Our Lady's CP School, Dartford

Penguins

Sea lover
Deep diver
Belly slider
Noise maker
Working waddler
Funny forever.

Jack Jukes (8)
Our Lady's CP School, Dartford

Celtic

C eltic is brilliant
E ven better that Chelsea
L ike Manchester Untied
T he top of the Scottish Premier League
I like them a lot
'C ause we will win the lot.

Fintan Cadden (8)
Our Lady's CP School, Dartford

Untitled

There once was a girl called Rose
Who had a really long nose.
She danced all night
Until it got light
And finally got time for a doze.

Hulya Yosma (9)
Our Lady's CP School, Dartford

My Friend Forever

E mily is a good friend
M y best friend forever
I like playing with her and
L ike her very much
Y ou are the best friend ever!

Mia Ridzwan (9)
Our Lady's CP School, Dartford

Roger And The Robber

Once there was a boy called Roger
Whose nickname was The Greatest Dodger.
One day someone took his toys
Then he heard a noise
And noticed it was the big robber.

Dean Gonzales (9)
Our Lady's CP School, Dartford

My New Puppy

P uppies are loving
U nbelievably cute
P uppies are small
P uppies can love each other
Y ou will always be my best puppy forever.

Emily Jeeves (9)
Our Lady's CP School, Dartford

Untitled

There once was a fat boy called Guts
Who always came home with cuts.
He ate and ate
But not from a plate
And that drove him completely nuts.

Joshua Ise (9)
Our Lady's CP School, Dartford

My Friend Kate

There once was a girl called Kate
Who got in one big state.
When she ate her dinner
She got thinner and thinner
And even licked the plate.

Sophie Glandfield (9)
Our Lady's CP School, Dartford

My Guppy

My guppy swims round straight and curvy
Fast, nippy and quick then hovering like a ship
He silently watches the other fish
Waiting patiently for the lid to open wide
So he can swim to the top and catch his prize.

Seán Ryan (8)
Our Lady's CP School, Dartford

The Ice

The ice is as hard as a wooden chair
And as shiny as my shoes
When I go in my car
And look out the window
All I see is ice.

Sarah Johnson (8)
Our Lady's CP School, Dartford

My Boy

There once was a boy called Spike
Who went on a very long hike.
He lost his way
Early that day
So decided to go by bike.

Ellie Atkins (9)
Our Lady's CP School, Dartford

Buffy

There once was a girl called Buffy
Who didn't know nothing.
They made her go to college
To gather more knowledge
And her brain came back all puffy.

Evan Page (8)
Our Lady's CP School, Dartford

My Teddy

T eddies are soft and cute
E very teddy is cuddly
D o everything with my teddy, even
D ine with my teddy, do
Y ou too?

Megan Draper (8)
Our Lady's CP School, Dartford

Friend

Peace maker
Joke teller
Work helper
Always there
Best friend.

Alexandra Lynn (9)
Our Lady's CP School, Dartford

Untitled

There was an old man from Peru
Who didn't know what to do.
He stood on a hill
Made himself ill
And died at seventy-two.

Alex Ojo (8)
Our Lady's CP School, Dartford

The Monkey

M onkeys are silly
O ld ones and young ones
N aughty ones
K ind ones
E ating fruit
Y elling in the jungle.

Rhys Branch (8)
Riverside Primary School, Rainham

Winter Is My Favourite Time Of Year

Winter is my favourite time of year because
Snow is soft and fluffy.
Winter is my favourite time of year because
Rain comes down like leaves.
Winter is my favourite time of year because
The fire is warm and cuddly.
Winter is my favourite time of year because
I can play in the snow.
Winter is my favourite time of year because
We all stay inside, cosy and hot.
Winter is my favourite time of year because
It is cold as the Arctic.
Winter is my favourite time of year because
I want it to be with me all of the time.

Olivia May Bridges (8)
Riverside Primary School, Rainham

A Snowman

Wet eyes
Icy hat
Cold mouth
Crunchy ice
Cold carrot
Icy body
Fat body
Cold snowman
Sitting in the snow.

Lucie Stewart (8)
Riverside Primary School, Rainham

A School Day

When you wake up and have to get ready for school
Don't pretend you're sick because you'll be missing out on all the
Running and playing,
Skipping and jumping,
Learning and listening,
Looking and drawing,
Writing and talking.
It's all fun, not just sitting and being told off.
It's really better than home when you're lying being sick,
                                          taking medicine
And you sometimes think you can play, watch TV and have fun stuff
But you just lie about.

Elisse Smith (8)
Riverside Primary School, Rainham

Cats!

Cats chase mice
Cats are noisy
Cats go mad
Cats go out
Cats eat jam
Cats are cute
Cats are cuddly
Cats sleep next to you
Cats are lovely.

Megan Wells (8)
Riverside Primary School, Rainham

My Teacher

My teacher always lends a hand.
My teacher is my friend.
When someone is mean she gives a shout.
But my teacher, my teacher is the best!
She cares for us; she loves us in every little way.
She listens to us; she takes good care of us when we treat her with respect.
That's why she's the best teacher in the world.

Jade Schopman (9)
Riverside Primary School, Rainham

The Squirrel

S quirrel running up a tree
Q uickly running on the grass,
U p and down,
I like the squirrel
R acing in the park
R acing in the woods,
E ating nuts
L ong, bushy tail.

Samantha O'Rourke (7)
Riverside Primary School, Rainham

Feelings

F eelings, feelings
E verywhere around you
E arly in the morning
L ittle people calling
I s a little child,
N oisy as can be
G oing to scare you, you
S cared me!

Lauryn Lelo (7)
Riverside Primary School, Rainham

Children

C hildren play
H ear babies when they cry
I n the bedroom playing together
L augh and giggle
D ance and dance
R eading with friends
E at lots of sweets
N ever break promises.

Sophie Clarkson (7)
Riverside Primary School, Rainham

A Winter Poem

Icicles as sharp as needles
Tree branches heavy with snow
Soft as a comfy pillow
Frost glittering like stars
Winter as cold as frozen ice
This is a happy joyful exciting time of year
Children having fun throwing snowballs and making giant fat snowmen.

Harley Burr (8)
Riverside Primary School, Rainham

Friends

F riends are funny
R eally nice
I like them because they
E njoy playing with me
N ever break promises
D oing things together
S ecrets never told.

Lucy Cordier (7)
Riverside Primary School, Rainham

My Dog Called Maisie

S he is called Maisie and has a
P retty face
A nd she has big black spots
N ever bites me
I love her for
E ver and ever and she
L ikes her tummy rubbed.

Nikita Skirth (7)
Riverside Primary School, Rainham

Winter

Winter is as cold as glittering ice.
I love winter because penguins are nice.
Winter is a great time of year.
Snowflakes fall from the sky.
People sit by the fire because it is so cold.
Snowball fights on the ice.
I love winter, it's so nice.

Melissa Godden (9)
Riverside Primary School, Rainham

Winter

Snow is as shiny as a diamond.
Snow falls down like raindrops.
Snowflakes fall down like hail.
Stay near the warm, cosy, hot fire and stay inside.
Snow is as cold as the Arctic.
Snow is fluffy and soft.
Snow falls down every winter.

Conor Murdoch (8)
Riverside Primary School, Rainham

Wintertime

Winter is freezing as icicles
The snow is cold as a snowman
Everything is frosty as snow
Rain is soggy as a puddle
It is snowing like rain
The snow is crunchy now.

Ryan Gordon (9)
Riverside Primary School, Rainham

My Dog Tom

T om is a black dog
O nce he was a puppy
M y dog, I love him.

Lauryn Hughes (7)
Riverside Primary School, Rainham

The Winter Poem

Winter is as cold as icicles
Snowman as slippery as freezing snowflakes
Snow as glittery as the moon
Icicles as frozen as snow
Snowmen are as white as icicles
I like winter most of all because it has snow.

Stanley McQueen (8)
Riverside Primary School, Rainham

The Scruffy Dog

A scruffy old dog sleeps in a bin
She is smelly and skinny
She got lost and couldn't find her home
So now she lives all alone
I wish I could help her
By making her mine.

Chloe Tilley (7)
Riverside Primary School, Rainham

Pear

P ears are green
E at them
A nd the juice
R uns down your chin.

Alfie Plumb (7)
Riverside Primary School, Rainham

Snowflakes

Snowflakes soft and glittery to light up the dark, dark night.
Sparkling while the cars go by and lighting up the road.
Everyone dancing with joy.
We love it when it snows and snowflakes are everywhere.
Come on everybody let's play in the snow.
It's still snowing, one, two, three, let's go!

Sinead Brown (8)
Riverside Primary School, Rainham

Baubles

Silky glass bauble
Shining
Twinkling on the tree
Golden bauble
Multicoloured bauble
Gold like a key.

Elysia Bradley (7)
Riverside Primary School, Rainham

Santa's Sack

Big, fat sack on Santa's sleigh
Elves cheering for the best time of year, Christmas!
Big, fat sack on Santa's back
Everyone is sleeping, waiting for Santa's home-made toys.

William Scales (7)
Riverside Primary School, Rainham

Poetry Explorers – Kent

The Like Poem

R abbits like jackets
A nd cows in a house
B ats like cats
B ut bats like hats
I like a lion
T o be like my mouse.

Marco Aicolino (8)
Riverside Primary School, Rainham

The Winter Poem

Icy on the ground, mushy on the snow
Breezy in the air, whoever knows.
Soggy shoes and misty sky,
Whoever knows where snow will lie.
Rainy floor and drenched clothes
Snowy head and cracked toes.

Tommy Hambrook (8)
Riverside Primary School, Rainham

A Tulip

A tulip is a summer flower that is red at night
It looks purple in the dark
Petals are smooth and sparkle like a star
A tulip glitters in the daylight like the big round sun.

Danielle Pymm (7)
Riverside Primary School, Rainham

Winter

Snow is as cold as the North Pole.
The snowflakes sparkle like stars.
The snow is as white as a baby polar bear.
Snowballs are as round as a ball.
Snow in the air floating everywhere.
Polar bear, a new one too, it is as cute as a cat.

Ellie Reeder (8)
Riverside Primary School, Rainham

The Tiger Cub

A tiger cub is small
A tiger cub is stripy
A tiger cub is orange and black
A tiger cub has a long tail
A tiger cub is cute.

Jack Briggs (7)
Riverside Primary School, Rainham

A Cold Day

Snow is as cold as the North Pole.
It is as thick and slippery as a wet log.
The winter snow is crunchy.
It is as glittery as shooting stars.
We all love wintertime!

Kieran Mallion (8)
Riverside Primary School, Rainham

Christmas Presents

I'm a box covered in a coloured wrapper with a toy inside
I was first delivered by the Wise Men
Now by Santa Claus
Elves make me all year
Working so the children can cheer.

Conor Sullivan (7)
Riverside Primary School, Rainham

Valentines

I wrote this poem just for you
Your valentines will come true.
Your hair is nice and eyes too
It's valentines, it's valentines
I love you!

Chloe-Jai Fendick (8)
Riverside Primary School, Rainham

Summer

The sun is bright in the sky
Bunnies jump high in summer
The flowers are colour in the air
The lake shining like a diamond
Summer is great and it's the best.

Charlotte O'Rourke (9)
Riverside Primary School, Rainham

The Winter Poem

Winter is cold as frozen, shivering ice
And we can have a snowball fight and make a big, fat snowman.
Winter is windy with fluffy, moving and furry, patterned clouds.
I like it because it gives us some breeze on our faces and blows
                                                                             our hair.

Shane Treeby (8)
Riverside Primary School, Rainham

TV Shows

I've watched 'Demons' once
'Doctor Who Confidential' a few times
'Doctor Who' lots of times
I like 'Tom & Jerry' but what I like better than television
Is my DS because it's better vision.

William Gardner (8)
Riverside Primary School, Rainham

Toys

T oys are everywhere
O n your floor
Y our bed is not used for
S leeping on no more.

Joanne Keating (8)
Riverside Primary School, Rainham

Books

Books I can read over and over again
Out in the garden, keeping me very quiet
Snow White is the book I'm reading
Wow, that book is amazing.

Thalia Burr (7)
Riverside Primary School, Rainham

Winter

The snow is as sparkling as the glittering shooting stars in the dark night.
The polar bears are as soft as a fluffy and comfy blanket.
We all love winter.

Leah Mai Harrison (8)
Riverside Primary School, Rainham

Winter

Icicles as sharp as needles
Frost glittering like stars
Winter as frozen ice.

Beau Hall
Riverside Primary School, Rainham

The Sea

A bandon ships
B ig boats
C urious curses
D ead bodies
E xtraordinary creatures
F antastic fish
G littery waterfalls
H orrendous beaches
I nternal destruction
J ealous jellyfish
K iller whales
L ots of limescale
M ost wonderful creature
N ight-time beauty
O ctopus
P irates stealing pearls
Q uiet sea
R ed blood
S itting and enjoying
T errorising sharks
U nderwater surprised
V iewing of the moon
W hales
X marks the spot
Y ellow
Z ooming dolphins.

Josh Saar (11)
Rosherville CE Primary School, Gravesend

The Dangerous Jungle

Lions loudly roaring
Gorillas quietly snoring
Rain heavily crashing
Apes viciously chest-bashing
Shakes quietly hissing
Wind wildly whistling
Green leaves rattling
Elephants' ears flapping
Deafening rapids flowing
Beautiful lizards glowing
Small creatures dawdling
Silver waterfall falling
That's the jungle
It's such a big bundle.

Yasmine Burrha (10)
Rosherville CE Primary School, Gravesend

Dolphins

D olphins can swim all the time because they have lots of energy
O ff they go on the blue wavy sea, they swim so perfectly
L ikes to play all day going over and through hoops
P eople throw delicious fish to them; they eat it up in no time
H appy dolphins get so excited by food and toys
I ll dolphins, just lie there all day long
N ot all dolphins are friendly
S ome are not nice!

Vikki Smith (9)
Rosherville CE Primary School, Gravesend

T-Rex

Ground rumbler
Claw slasher
Meat shredder
Fast runner
Human eater
Bone cruncher
Bone breaker
Bad swimmer
Raging temper
Meat grinder
Teeth slasher
Run for your life, it's a T-rex.

Jamie-Leigh Yardley (11)
Rosherville CE Primary School, Gravesend

Space

As I was zooming up to space
The breeze was rushing through my face
There were lots of shining stars
I almost could see the planet Mars!
The sun is so bright, Earth was out of sight
Oh, space is so quiet.

Emily Jane Ringer (9)
Rosherville CE Primary School, Gravesend

Poetry Explorers – Kent

Space

S aturn is a glamorous planet
P luto is made of gigantic rocks
A liens get hit by rapid asteroids
C omets gliding across the sky at two hundred miles per hour
E arth whirling around and around.

Tegan Rai (9)
Rosherville CE Primary School, Gravesend

The Sea

The
Sea is
Rough,
Blue with
Lots of waves
High, small
And medium
All coming
Towards me
The waves
Were so
Big
But
They
Have
Gone.

Keeley Stocker (11)
St William of Perth School, Rochester

Meteors In Space

M agical moments in marvellous space
E xhilaration fills the hearts of every astronaut
T he spectacular view of the whizzing rocks
E nhancing their show as they twirl and bow
O ne more leap for mankind
R ushing quickly to reach their destination
S pecial and breathtaking

I magination becomes reality and reality becomes imagination
N o boundaries, no barriers, just open space

S hooting stars bring luck to Earth
P romises made to visit the moon
A bility to roam the galaxy feeling relaxed
C apsules floating freely and calmly
E xcited astronauts raise the flag proudly.

Amy Abbotson (11)
St William of Perth School, Rochester

My Emotions

I felt overjoyed in the park,
running freely through the grassy field!

I felt broken when I fell over
on to the hard, slippery broken ice.

I felt excited when I got my
Nintendo DS for the first time ever!

I felt homesick when I left my mum
to go to camp for a week.

Heather McMahon (10)
St William of Perth School, Rochester

The Jungle

The jungle is lush,
The animals are sleeping
In the green jungle.

They are now awake,
Drinking the crystal water
In the green jungle.

The moth is flying,
The luscious birds are singing
In the green jungle.

I will miss this place,
This place is the green jungle.
I won't forget you.

Charlotte Byrne (11)
St William of Perth School, Rochester

The Sea

Wishing, washing,
never stopping.
Free to roam wherever it wants.
Calm and pleasant it may be,
but sometimes it's not as pretty.
Rapid and aggressive it
turns out to be.
But then it turns
back to normal.
Back to smooth
and gentle.

Eve Rushforth (11)
St William of Perth School, Rochester

Jungle

The jungle is lush,
The animals are swimming,
And it is quiet!

The lions are sleeping,
And the sloth and the moth,
And it is quiet!

The leaves are green,
Lots of animals are sleeping,
So be quiet please!

This is the jungle,
The animals are singing,
Goodbye and take care!

Sarah Louise Ireland (10)
St William of Perth School, Rochester

Bubbling Anger

I feel like I am going to bubble up and burst.
Feeling I need to spill out with all of my burdens.
I need to find a place where
I can just scream and no one hear me.
'Argh!'

I let it out
I run as if my life depends on it.
I feel so free.
Letting the troubles be let loose.
'Fffrrreee!'

Rachel Narborough (10)
St William of Perth School, Rochester

The Jungle

The jungle is loud,
and the colourful birds fly.
This is the jungle.

The animals feel
like they are active now.
This is the jungle.

So come here right now,
and enjoy their playfulness.
This is the jungle!

It's time to go home,
say goodbye to the creatures.
That was the jungle.

Francesca Knight (11)
St William of Perth School, Rochester

The Dragon

The dragon slept, the dragon dreamed
Of what was to come.
A knight in shining armour came
And fought him and won.

And then it occurred to the dragon,
And then it occurred to him,
Why in fairy stories
Does the knight always win?

Katherine Knight (11)
St William of Perth School, Rochester

The Sea

The
Sea
Icy, blue,
Invincible,
Smashing,
Crashing on the
Cold, hard rocks.
Making everyone
Thrilled.
The
Brilliant
Sea.

John Paul Swain (10)
St William of Perth School, Rochester

Buzzz!

Buzzing, buzzing like a bee
I can hear, but nobody else can you see.
I walk out of school feeling worried.
I tell my mum but she can do
Nothing about it you see.
Later and it's getting worse
Aching, baking hot and beeping.
Screaming for help!
I'm hot and bothered,
Painful and whinging.
I should have got my earache
Seen to earlier.

Libby Godfrey (10)
St William of Perth School, Rochester

The Jungle

The crystal water
the singing is loud
the jungle is dead.

The army are here
to kill all the animals
I am so sorry,
the jungle is dead.

Some don't like them.
All the animals can't run away
the land will be starved
the jungle is dead.

Michael Polley (11)
St William of Perth School, Rochester

Godzilla

Godzilla roars as he destroys,
Making such an unbearable noise.
Doors are closed tight,
As he flees into the night.

Shops sell their toy figures,
As the police pull their triggers.
For the boys he's such a hero,
As he decreases the population to zero.

Cameron Payas (10)
St William of Perth School, Rochester

The Sea

The sea is strong, aggressive,
Noisy, blue, invincible,
Vicious, non-stopping,
Terrific.
The waves crash into the rocks,
With people playing and having fun.
The waves go in and out.

Jack Waller (10)
St William of Perth School, Rochester

The Bullies

The bullies of the block,
They beat you up, steal and spit on you.
Everyone fears them, even me!
The thugs try to steal from me,
I tell them, 'No!'
I am petrified,
I will rest in peace!

Stephen McSwiney (10)
St William of Perth School, Rochester

Poetry Explorers – Kent

The Shark

As he hunts for his prey,
As he swims quicker and quicker and quicker
Because he's not getting any thinner.
It's his hunger, you're his hunger, you're his dinner.
Round and round he'll circle you,
Until you drown and then he'll eat you.

Joseph Smith (10)
St William of Perth School, Rochester

Space

S himmering stars lighting up the night sky
P lanets spinning, orbiting the sun
A lien invasion, quick, what should we do?
C lear the area, go and hide in the craters
E arth, our planet, home!

Georgina Wolski (10)
St William of Perth School, Rochester

Cats

They curl round your feet,
They hang round the street,
They eat from your bin, or their Felix tin,
They curl up on your lap and decide to have a nap,
They play with the mouse and leave dead ones outside your house!

Abbi De La Hoyde (10)
St William of Perth School, Rochester

My Space Poem

S tars gleaming in the sky
P utting light in the night
A stronauts bravely travelling in a place with no atmosphere
C omets going at the speed of light
E ndured meteors, knights of non-atmosphere.

Mitchell Ekundayo Elba (10)
St William of Perth School, Rochester

My Family

F avourite thing in my life
A lways out and having fun
M y best friends
I nvented happiness
L ike to keep me safe
Y ou will stay in my head

P erfect and furry
E ntertaining and funny
T reat to have
S ometimes a bit expensive at the vets.

S ometimes annoying
I rritate each other
S ometimes loving
T ease each other
E ncourage fights
R eally wind each other up
S miling.

Nicola Freer
Stone St Mary's School, Greenhithe

My Friends Poem

My friend is from Mars,
He drives blue and black cars,
At his best,
He makes an enormous mess,
We will be friends,
Till the end.

My friend is from Neptune,
He plays a recorder,
All out of tune,
At the concert,
He forgot it,
So no one remembers the tune.

My friend is from Saturn,
She makes lovely patterns,
All around the room,
If you try to stop her,
She'll give you a clobber,
But don't slobber.

My friend is from Jupiter,
He's a superstar,
He can run so far,
Without a car,
He flew to Mars,
But he's my superstar.

My friend is from Venus
And you should have seen us.

Liam Massey
Stone St Mary's School, Greenhithe

Teacher

Teacher shouts
Teacher knows
Teacher smiles
The whole school blows

He is always right
He gives people a fright
He knows what to say
Like, 'Go out and play'

Teacher shouts
Teacher knows
Teacher smiles
The whole school blows

When someone is bad
He gets mad
When someone is good
He praises them like he should

Teacher shouts
Teacher knows
Teacher smiles
The whole school blows

You might have guessed
He is the best
He likes baseball caps
He is Mr Apps!

Ellenor Palmer (9)
Stone St Mary's School, Greenhithe

Seasons

Spring is the first, always calm
Never scary, no alarm
Its warm embrace wraps around you
Let spring last, no time to lose.

Summer is the best for everyone
All enjoying the hot, orange sun
Calm beaches, waves to the shore
Love is shown, they want some more.

Autumn, crunchy, crispy leaves
The calm breeze against the trees
Jumping in leaf piles is so much fun
The cold nights have just begun.

Winter, the last, brings fun and despair
Snow-white blanket everywhere
The cold, starry nights, out of sight
Lullabies are sung, whispering, 'Goodnight.'

Glenys Adelusi
Stone St Mary's School, Greenhithe

Dragons

D angerous creatures that can fly
R eptiles that can breathe fire
A rrogant and scaly creatures
G one, but are they really extinct?
O r did they really exist?
N o knight's story would be complete without one
S cary or not, you decide?

Jordan Card (9)
Stone St Mary's School, Greenhithe

My Rabbit

(In remembrance of my rabbit called Roger who died on Sunday 12th April, 2008. We miss Roger very much)

Smokey-blue
Burrow-digger
Nose-twitcher
Carrot-cruncher
Hay-nibbler
Guinea pig-lover
Tail-shaker
Warm-licker
Hole-maker
Biscuit-pincher
Wire-chewer
Tea-drinker
Lap-sitter
Plant-wrecker
A naughty, but nice.

Courtney Price (10)
Stone St Mary's School, Greenhithe

Chocolate

Chocolate,
Brown, sticky,
Sucking, melting, chomping,
The delicious taste of the brown stuff,
Crunching, chewing, enjoying,
Fresh, juicy
Fruit.

Josh Lewis (9)
Stone St Mary's School, Greenhithe

Poetry Explorers – Kent

The Tar Pits

If you go down to the tar pits today,
You'll be in for a big surprise,
Because if you go down to the tar pits, to the tar pits today,
You'll see where T-rex hides!

So if you go down to the tar pits today,
You won't live to say your goodbyes,
If you go down to the tar pits today,
For you the end of the world will be nigh.

Because if you go down to the tar pits today,
You will be long neck stew,
Or triceratops cashew,
Or even worse, T-rex poo!

So if you don't want to be in any of these,
Stay in your holes, nests or trees,
So stay in the bushes or your nesting grounds please.

Ciaran Jones
Stone St Mary's School, Greenhithe

Trees

Brown, green leaves
Give us oxygen to live
Helps us live our lives
Trees.

Chocolate
Brown, crunchy
If you eat lots of it
You might get a tummy ache.

Mylim Taylor-Gray (9)
Stone St Mary's School, Greenhithe

A Poem About Cars

There are lots of cars all around
Different shapes and sizes can be found
Cars can be slow or can be fast
There were very slow cars in the past
Cars are big, small and sometimes flash
If they are fast, you need to make sure you don't crash.

To drive on the road you need tax
Insurance and an MOT
If you do not have these, in trouble you would be
To drive a car you need to take a driving test
It's very hard and you need to do your best
When I'm older I would like a big, red, shiny car
So I can go for a long drive with my family, very far.

Jack Coburn (10)
Stone St Mary's School, Greenhithe

Snow

Snow is wonderful
Snow is fun-filled and playful
Snow is brilliant
Snow is cool
And every child likes it
And when they see it
They get all excited
And straight away
They shout out
'Can I go out now?'

Gregory Hassall (9)
Stone St Mary's School, Greenhithe

Spring

It's time for spring
The flowers are king
And all the bugs are out.

The trees are tall
It's a wonderful time
And all the bugs are out.

The birds are out
It is a fantastic time
And all the bugs are out.

Everything is in bloom.
What a view!

Corina Fox
Stone St Mary's School, Greenhithe

Butterflies

B utterflies are colourful
U nderneath the sun
T hey are in their chrysalis
T hey are waiting for the time to come when they can come out
E very butterfly doesn't wish they were a caterpillar again
R ed, blue, yellow and brown are the most common colours
                                                          on a butterfly
F lowers are what they drink from
L ovely creatures are butterflies
I think butterflies are beautiful
E very butterfly eats leaves when they are a caterpillar
S ome butterflies are the same.

Chloe Newton (10)
Stone St Mary's School, Greenhithe

My Pet Brother Kennings

Phone-hogger
Football-lover
Mess-maker
Fashion-worshipper
Chocolate-fan
Remote-stealer
Laughter-maker
Shoe-seller
Money-spender
My big bro.

Chloe Lawrence (9)
Stone St Mary's School, Greenhithe

Hospital

(I wrote this when I was being treated at Lewisham Hospital)

H elping others is what we do best,
O ver the country to the test
S pecial people everywhere
P eople unwell and people that care
I n the ward tucked up in beds
T ogether they want to rest their heads
A ll the nurses can help you too
L ewisham is for me and you.

Robyn King (9)
Stone St Mary's School, Greenhithe

Moonlight

M any miles above
O ver us it watches at night
O n task it is, when it gets dark
N ight-time is its time to shine
L igfht it gives to us at night
I n the night sky is where it stands
G ives us light
H as a different shape every night
T wilight it appears as a shiny, silver ball.

Grace Johnson
Stone St Mary's School, Greenhithe

The Goldfish

I have a goldfish called Squiggy
When he swims around it makes me feel dizzy
No noise and no sound
He sucks pebbles up off the ground
And he always looks like he's busy
But when he's been fed
He must feel like lead
As he sinks to the bottom of his bowl.

Toby Hooker (10)
Stone St Mary's School, Greenhithe

Diamonds

D azzle like the sunlight
I nteresting colours when in the sunshine
A re forever
M y favourite jewel
O n my wish list
N ecklace and bracelets
D irty when first found
S hining like sparkling stars.

Jordan Burgess
Stone St Mary's School, Greenhithe

Acrostic Poem

R ubbish may be reused,
E veryone need not be confused.
C an be kept for another day,
Y ours to keep, not throw away.
C an't you see, it all makes sense,
L et's reuse and save some pence.
E njoy your life, it's not a sin,
D on't chuck all things in the bin.

James Harding (10)
Stone St Mary's School, Greenhithe

Monster

M ostly seen in the dark
O nly real in your imagination
N ight-time they strike
S care you in your dreams
T ell yourself they're not real
E very night they give you a fright
R un, run, run.

Cameron Rose (10)
Stone St Mary's School, Greenhithe

My Life

My life, my life,
My wonderful life.
My life, my life,
What shall I decide?
My life, my life,
I love my life.

Narayan Chatha (9)
Stone St Mary's School, Greenhithe

Happy

H aving a laugh with my friend
A nd enjoying my family
P laying tricks on everyone
P laying football and learning to be a good goalkeeper
Y ou can make me happy by being my friend.

Matthew Jones (10)
Stone St Mary's School, Greenhithe

I Like Maths

I like maths, it is fun,
My favourite number is twenty-one,
Numbers, angles and fractions too,
I like maths, how about you?

Liam Reed (10)
Stone St Mary's School, Greenhithe

Stars

S hining bright in the night sky
T winkling high above
A lways lighting up the world
R eally precious.

Amy Manchester (9)
Stone St Mary's School, Greenhithe

Hail

Hail is a bitter, egocentric and spitting man
Who thinks he's better than everyone else.
Moving swiftly and in rhythm, he's a hunting assassin.
Hands out, claws at the ready.
Knocking on the door and running away.

Spitting down on people he thinks are puny and make him angry.
His spit feels like a thousand shards of sharp cutting glass,
Which get harder depending on how angry he is.
Sucking up air then spitting it out makes him feel omnipotent.
Creating winds and hail is his favourite type of sport.

Watching all the little people running from his power
Has made him selfish after all these years.
Controlling the wind and rain in his glory.
Sharing with nobody is his goal, so the glory is only his.

Roaring with laughter he is a wolf howling with the wind.
Shaking with his laughter his icicle clothes rattle like a xylophone.
When he gets bored of watching people run,
The storm dies down and he lets out the sun.

Rebecca Artemis Preston (11)
Whitfield & Aspen School, Dover

Lightning

Striking through misty paths on a cold winter's day,
High up in the sky just like fireworks,
Cavorting around the sky like a gigantic fly,
Flashing like a flickering light bulb,
Lighting up the sky everywhere it goes.

Abbey Roberts (11)
Whitfield & Aspen School, Dover

Hail

Hands clatter on the floor.
Sprinkling on green grass.
Legs splashing in puddles.
Thumping infinitely on windows.

Dropping at a rhythmic pace.
Hands and claws out at the ready.
Knocking on the roof at a rapid pace.
Falling sharp glass hitting the fields.

Beating on everyone,
Searching for its prey.
Seizing and clutching, holding on,
Scratching, punching; his enemy is gone.

Fists ready to tap on doors.
Getting angrier as he gets harder.
Turning more selfish as he drops on roads.
Melting into water as the sun shines.
He's gone now, but he'll soon return.

Thrishali Sumanasekera (10)
Whitfield & Aspen School, Dover

The Snail

I'm a slug with a smooth spiralling crash helmet.
Yep, you guessed it!
I'm a snail. I move slowly with ma house in my helmet.
A bed, a gym, you name it, I got it.
Now us snails like to come out at night.
So we can move as slowly as we like!

Tom Wood (10)
Whitfield & Aspen School, Dover

The Storm

Wind is sighing,
Being whipped by the rain,
Lightning cavorting across the sky,
Thunder roaring again and again.

Sprightly hail sprinting across the sky,
Lightning's face; from a zenith unseen,
Kicking down buildings, bridges and trees,
Appearing everywhere, you are never appeased.

Thunder's song is an opera on its own,
Always singing his endless song,
He knows where you're hiding so he makes you hear,
His mighty voice is prodigious and strong.

Rain's rivalry with hail is weakened,
Its pride and strength has been fatally wounded,
Fingering its way through the congregation's of clouds,
A shining face peers through the darkness.

Benjamin Kieran Harris (11)
Whitfield & Aspen School, Dover

Lightning And Thunder

Striking through dark clouds
Its blood-curdling voice from Hell
Fingertips raiding through the gloomy dark
A blazing, undestroyable flame!

His face is an unexpected source that hits Earth
A blazing flame building into a booming giant
Slaughtering its prey through a sharp-clawed chainsaw.

Carl Hermon (10)
Whitfield & Aspen School, Dover

The Sun

Arms sway gradually through the day,
Padding feet walk,
But you never hear them,
Contentedly works with the clouds.

Face lights up like a young girl's,
Who has just got a Nintendo Wii,
Staring down on us she sneers,
But she shines so brightly,
You can't see her facial features.

Children playing timidly as she watches them,
Having fun all day long,
Participating in a game at the beach,
Having so much fun in the hot, hot sun!

Chloe Burr (11)
Whitfield & Aspen School, Dover

Rain Is Falling

The rain is screaming
Striking the old oak tree
As its tight-fisted hands hit the ground repeatedly
One by one, the little army scurries down the drainpipe
Ready to regroup to fight with the light.

The gentle skin
Sounds like someone tapping a desk
Hitting the window for all to hear
As it dies, the rain will rise
To be born again and to fall again.

Toby Clayton (10)
Whitfield & Aspen School, Dover

Poetry Explorers – Kent

The Snail

I love a treat,
I'm a vegetarian and I like to munch,
I am slow and steady,
Some people call me a garden pest,
I travel all over the world,
I like the damp,
I can be seen near a pond,
I have cousins that can grow to 30cms.

I have to be very careful,
Or I might get eaten,
Good job I have my shell for protection.

Uh-oh, time to run,
See you tomorrow if I don't die.

Callum Tanton (9)
Whitfield & Aspen School, Dover

Snail Poem

I'm Bob the slippery, slimy snail.
I love the damp but not the cold.
My home is my spiral shell.
Inside I don't have much.
Only a bed with some grass for a duvet.
I have four eyes which are my antennae.
I have big enemies, birds, they eat me.
We are all vegetarians
So don't worry people.
Nothing to be scared of then.

Lewis Bird (9)
Whitfield & Aspen School, Dover

Snowflakes

As the tender newborn snow
Peacefully enters the world
With its delicate and frosty skin
As cold as cold can be.

With one touch of warmth
Will change her heart forever
As she slowly crawls and dances
To wherever she wishes to go.

She always sparkles and glistens
Until she meets her one true love
Unless she dies of old age
And carefully falls to the ground.

Jaimee Baldwin (10)
Whitfield & Aspen School, Dover

Thunder And Lightning

She cavorts in the sky
Her hair lights up everything she passes
Pleasing everyone and everything
Sizzling like a sausage, she strikes here and there

Fighting like a wounded animal, his majesty keeps on flashing
And her royal highness keeps on striking
To make themselves champ of the sky
Zigzagging across it, dodging each other's traps!
He then opens a new door, revealing a cloudy storm
Making everyone miserable
As the blue sky is substituted with a storm.

Beth Roberts (10)
Whitfield & Aspen School, Dover

The Hail

She's a criminal breaking into everyone's cars,
Shattering on windows as she falls,
Spitting in anger through her rusty skies,
Not caring where she falls.

That icy mind of hers,
Cold and unworried, mean and sharp,
Targeting her pathway from the clouds,
Stealing the happy thoughts left in the world.

Her sharp but shiny body,
She hurls herself rapidly in desperation for war,
Knocking everyone out of her way,
How ghastly is that evil witch?

Georgia Finnis (11)
Whitfield & Aspen School, Dover

The Graveyard

She stood there in the graveyard
Her long dark hair swaying in the moonlight
Her bloodstained dress showed how inhuman she was.

Ghost-like face showing no emotion but a single tear
She stood there staring with her cold blue eyes at the sky
Her thin blue lips repeating the same words, SOS over and over again.

If you were even a metre near her, a shiver would go up your spine
You would shout, but she would not move
She screamed and she was gone.

Elisabeth Hall (10)
Whitfield & Aspen School, Dover

The Sun

Her fingertips sway in the light breeze throughout the day,
Cavorting across the sky,
Providing jubilant light,
Breaking the clouds up as she goes.

Taking pleasure in seeing children playing,
Face lighting up the blue sky,
Smiling as she shines,
Relaxing in the slight breeze.

As the day ends her sunset is appealing,
Loitering down to rest,
Letting the moon take over,
Waiting for morning to come again.

Amelia Ward (10)
Whitfield & Aspen School, Dover

The Rain

Shimmers and sparkles as it falls
Like a scatter of crystal clear diamonds
Falls from the sky like a million people crying
Plop-plop as it hits the ground, its bones shatter to pieces.

Sounds like little elves tapping on the roof
Showers are soft but downpours hit the ground with hatred in the eye
Silent and swift as it moves through the air,
Like an assassin closing in on its target,
Comes down as an army invading the land.

Daniel Marshall (11)
Whitfield & Aspen School, Dover

Snow

Slowly she moves through the forest
Her hands as cold as ice
Snow in her hair and nails
Fingertips all smooth and tender.

Walking at a steady pace
Skin all frosty and pale
Hearing magical creatures
As she drifts through the night.

Clothes made out of snow
Tears dropping in her hand
Speaks with a cold breath
As he vanishes in thin air.

Melodie Letchford (10)
Whitfield & Aspen School, Dover

My Brother Braden

My little brother Braden is a little bear
Growling for his dinner in the night's glare
He's a bouncy bed which is easily said
He's a good tune blowing in the wind
He's a funhouse in the boring street
He is a tasty chocolate bar
Always getting bitten because he's so sweet
My little brother Braden doesn't change a bit
Spring, summer, autumn, winter has no effect.

Brendan Foottit (10)
Whitfield & Aspen School, Dover

Thunderclouds

Moving its black body through the sky
Knocking on every door it meets
Arms squished, legs crumpled
As it moves through the sky.

Roars every minute, eager to start
Scaring everybody or thing it flies past
A black widow rushing through the street
Hurrying through the shops.

A black body moving and changing through the midnight sky
Spinning around the moon as it runs
Making it dark, killing the night
The thunderclouds float around.

Samuel Edwards (10)
Whitfield & Aspen School, Dover

My Snail Poem

I know I'm not the prettiest creature
But that doesn't bother me
I live in a golden shell
Sometimes it doesn't protect me
Because people stand or tread on us
Which really hurts
So that's why I come out at night
It's called nocturnal
That's what I am - nocturnal.

Jasmine Graham (9)
Whitfield & Aspen School, Dover

The Thundercloud

Arms tugging, legs pushing
Cavorting across the sky
She runs over the fields
Bellowing out loud.

Fists clenched
Hair holding her back
Stars scraping her spine
Pompous in her ways.

Fingers flinching
Toes cut by trees
Gracefully taking leaps
As the thundercloud moves along the sky.

Alex Riley (10)
Whitfield & Aspen School, Dover

The Snow Queen

Walking slowly and steadily,
Reaching out to touch,
Breathing with a cool breath,
Her skin soft and white.

Fingertips reaching for the ground,
Eyes looking downwards,
Aware of the sun reflecting,
Melting her talented work.

Danielle Cole (11)
Whitfield & Aspen School, Dover

My English Teacher

She's a comfy bed that you can snuggle into.
She's a very spectacular sofa ready for action.
She's a very sensitive baby chicken ready to peck.
She's a really shy rabbit tucked in her hutch.
She is the Canterbury Cathedral with her pointy nose.
She's the London Eye that storms up ahead.
She's a very angry, barking dog.
She's a very crunchy bit of bacon just as it's being fried.
She's a very hard chunk of meat, always hard to beat.
She's a very dark morning, always pretty grumpy.
She's a very big motorbike, always revving its engine.
Of course, it's Mrs Williams.

Ashley Baldwin (11)
Whitfield & Aspen School, Dover

Snowflake

He falls out from the sky with a tiny chill in his heart.
The newborn snow doesn't make a sound.
The little flake crawls and dances to wherever he wishes.
His little blank skin is as fragile as a feather.

As he takes his first twirl he sparkles in the daylight.
He leaps and jumps, twirls and spins as happy as can be.
He whirls and twirls till he meets the flake of his dreams.
The love of his life warms his heart forever.

He's coming to the end of his life with his love.
Getting closer and closer to the dazzling snow.
He takes his last few twirls and . . . gone forever.

Robyn Davison (11)
Whitfield & Aspen School, Dover

Raindrops

The pitter-patter of small feet
They hit the ground in despair
They come in armies of a million
And have slick hair.

Hands filled with drizzle
Hair dripping with water
Feet wet and damp
They fill the puddles again.

Dylan Proudlock-Damms (10)
Whitfield & Aspen School, Dover

My Brother

He is as sly as a fox
He's a bouncy bed
My brother is soft bread
He is as charming as a New York scene
A cold, snowy winter
He is a noisy, banging drum
He is someone I can look up to

He is my brother.

Josh Fagg (11)
Whitfield & Aspen School, Dover

The Thunder And Lightning

Striding through the misty sky
He's parsimonious and repulsive,
His cold, cruel fingertips sending a chill down people's spines,
Hissing at passers-by.

Zigzagging in every direction,
His bashing, crashing footsteps,
The deafening echo of his voice leaves you paralysed,
His spirit brings darkness all around him.

Gaby Northcott (11)
Whitfield & Aspen School, Dover

Rain

A snap and a crackle on the window.
Swimming through the sea of dreams.
Travelling down faces as tears of sadness.
Walking through the sewers of desolation.

Coming in an army of millions.
Jumping through the sky.
Hitting the ground in depression.
With skin smoother than air.

William Okou (11)
Whitfield & Aspen School, Dover

People Poem

She's a bouncy bed,
She's a roaring lion,
The taste of France,
Always sings like Britney Spears,
Like a spicy curry,
A warm summer,
Best of all
A great teacher!

Jordan Bale (11)
Whitfield & Aspen School, Dover

The Snail

I'm just an ordinary snail.
I only have one back.
I am a very bad garden pest.
When it is dark, I come out and leave a glimmering trail.
I come out and mess about.
My speed is slow but careful.
Am I a crunchy treat? You decide!
It is up to you!

Thomas Nunn (10)
Whitfield & Aspen School, Dover

The Snail

I saw a snail with a spiral shell
Slowly and gently moving along,
He left a slimy but sparkly trail,
I wish I had a home on my back,
I wonder what he's thinking,
He could be thinking that I'm a giant,
But I know what I'm thinking,
I think he's tiny.

Matthew Ashbee (9)
Whitfield & Aspen School, Dover

People Poem – Ben, My Cousin

My cousin Ben
Is an exciting toy box full of presents
He is a mad new puppy entering the world
He is a new exhilarating ride at a theme park
He is a famous guitar player
He is a hyperactive, shaken up Coke bottle
He is summer, full of fun and surprises
A soft, cuddly cushion.

Amy Kansy (10)
Whitfield & Aspen School, Dover

Lightning Strikes

The sound of echoing thunder booming through your ears
Fingers rapidly flowing down its body
Arms are as hot as fire on a sunny day
Body covering the Earth and bringing darkness everywhere he looks
Rain falling down from him, flooding the omnipotent seas
Ruining days out at the beach
He comes when you least expect him
No friend of the sun.

Thomas Ashbee (11)
Whitfield & Aspen School, Dover

My Sister Caitlin

My sister is an angry fireplace burning in the room.
In the morning she's a cat dozing silently.
Caitlin is a toy shop sitting on the busy street.
She's a recorder squeaking in the classroom.
She's a cheeseburger waiting to be eaten.
She's spring to winter changing her moods.
Caitlin is a Coca-Cola can, shaken and fizzy.
She is a sparkler, ready to go off.

Alice Payne (10)
Whitfield & Aspen School, Dover

My Grandad

My grandad is a toy box full of fun,
A cuddly puppy, warm to the touch,
A cool, new theme park ready to go,
He's birds tweeting in the bush,
A bottle of fizzy water, calm, also mad,
He's summer fun, full of sun,
My grandad is a ghost train full of surprises.

Hannah Gumbley (10)
Whitfield & Aspen School, Dover

My Sister

Jessica is a springy bed, but cute,
She's an active monkey,
She is friendly France,
The sound of a cute puppy,
A lovely delicious roast dinner,
The sunny summertime
And the smell of a red rose.

Georgina Edmonds (11)
Whitfield & Aspen School, Dover

My Mum

She's the glowing embers in the bottom of a large fireplace,
A dawdling duck quacking for food,
My mum is a pretty princess in Turkey,
An angel singing a lullaby,
She's a bowl of strawberries in fresh cream,
She's spring as the flowers grow,
She's a coffee machine, constantly on the go.

Jessie Smissen (10)
Whitfield & Aspen School, Dover

My Sister

She's a jazzy leather sofa,
She's a sly little fox,
Buckingham Palace standing tall and proud,
A sharp bang of a loud drum,
The pop of a bubblegum,
The bright summer's sun, always warm,
The *tooooot!* of a steam train.

Aaron Edward Langley (10)
Whitfield & Aspen School, Dover

Mr Cook

He's a chair, hard but soft,
A monkey, clever and smart,
London, busy and exciting,
A golden lion, loud and roaring,
A colourful salad, healthy and smart,
He's a warm summer's day, always kind
A racing car, racing for victory.

Ellie Tomkinson (9)
Whitfield & Aspen School, Dover

My Sister Chelsea

She's a bed with no hardness,
Chelsea is an energetic cheetah,
She's a playground full of excitement,
An elephant stomping around,
A pea always looking small and being green,
She's midnight, fast asleep,
A pink rose smelling perfect.

Bethany Whitehead (9)
Whitfield & Aspen School, Dover

The Snail

I was slithering along a leaf,
Being a wonderful pest,
But I hate it when big weird giants stand on us,
What is even worse than that,
Is when French people eat us
And serve us up as a wonderful lunch.
Whatever can they see in snails and wine?

Philip O'Flaherty (10)
Whitfield & Aspen School, Dover

My Dad

My dad is a never-ending grandfather clock.
A giraffe who can reach up to the stars.
A beach with a rough tide.
He's a drum kit, banging all the time.
My dad's midday, always blocking light.

Aimee Martin (9)
Whitfield & Aspen School, Dover

The Snail

Ponderously climbing my tights on the clothes line,
Making them all slimy and gooey,
I must have picked off a whole family,
I put them in a huge bucket in my car,
I drove to the woods and put them safely on the ground.

Leigha Mills (11)
Whitfield & Aspen School, Dover

Young Writers Information

We hope you have enjoyed reading this book - and that you will continue to enjoy it in the coming years.

If you like reading and writing poetry drop us a line, or give us a call, and we'll send you a free information pack.

Alternatively if you would like to order further copies of this book or any of our other titles, then please give us a call or log onto our website at www.youngwriters.co.uk

Young Writers Information
Remus House
Coltsfoot Drive
Peterborough
PE2 9JX
(01733) 890066